The Executive's Guide

Successful

to ^ MRP II

The Executive's Guide

Successful

to MRP II

Oliver W. Wight

Oliver Wight Limited Publications, Inc.   Prentice-Hall, Inc.
P. O. Box 278   Englewood Cliffs, N.J.
Williston, VT 05495

ISBN 0-13-294249-6

Printed in the United States of America
The Book Press, Brattleboro, VT.

Table of Contents

Foreword

We will, undoubtedly, look back on the 1980's as the decade of the new industrial revolution. We saw our radio industry, our television industry, and our small appliance industry invaded by the Japanese, and didn't pay much attention. But when they brought us to our knees in our own automobile industry, we suddenly realized that our claim to be number one in manufacturing was being challenged.

By 1980, articles and talks called for the "reindustrialization of America." Productivity became a pervasive theme.

Manufacturing Resource Planning (MRP II) had evolved, meanwhile, out of Material Requirements Planning (MRP) into a company game plan. And the successful users demonstrated that these tools could be used to raise the level of professionalism in running our manufacturing businesses dramatically.

This book is a brief guide for the executive who would like to know more about MRP and MRP II, or the executive who has been educated and would like a refresher. It is not, obviously, a substitute for a formal education experience; it is a guide.

It won't take that long to read it cover to cover, and I hope you will. But the book was intended, also, as a brief, handy reference for the executive. As the subject comes to mind, you can refer back to the appropriate chapter.

This book is written in question and answer format. The questions are not contrived. They are based on my discussions with several thousand executives every year at our classes, at talks, and while consulting. Their contributions to my thinking, as well as those of my closest associates: Dave Garwood, Walt Goddard, Darryl Landvater - and, of course, Joan - must be acknowledged.

The terms MRP (Material Requirements Planning), Closed Loop MRP, and MRP II (Manufacturing Resource Planning) are discussed in Chapter 1. Note that throughout the book where it isn't important to distinguish between them, the term MRP is used generically just for the sake of simplicity. Usually the meaning is conveyed by the content of the sentence, just as we speak of New York and sometimes mean Manhattan, all the boroughs of New York, or New York State, without specifically defining which we mean every time we use the term.

I sincerely hope this book helps you on your "MRP journey."

Oliver W. Wight
Blodgett Landing, NH
December, 1981.

"Why Didn't MRP II Make the Wall Street Journal?"

OW   It does all the time.

Exec   Come on, Ollie. The Wall Street Journal never heard of MRP II - and if they did, they would probably think it was some kind of a computer system!

OW   But they do write about it. Didn't you read about the company that had to restate earnings because of an inventory shrinkage?

Exec   Which one? That happens all the time!

OW   How about our need for better productivity - or the fact that the Japanese work better as a team than we do?

Exec   I must say I'm getting a little tired of this Japanese stuff, but teamwork is something we sure could do better.

OW   Remember the company that took a long strike because their employees got sick of chronic overtime?

Exec   I know who you mean. They suffered terrible financial repercussions.

OW   How about the cash flow problem at the company that evidently didn't know how to gear production to sales and had to sell off their inventory at distress prices?

Exec   But the journal didn't mention MRP II in these articles, did they?

OW   No, they didn't. And when they talked about the performance at Black & Decker, Cameron Iron Works, Tennant Company and others that are Class A MRP II users, they didn't mention the credit their management gives to having these better tools either.

Exec   I hear your point, but why pick on the Wall Street Journal?

OW   Would you have preferred Forbes? Seriously,
      I'm just trying to illustrate the point that these
      business journals see what is on the surface, but
      they really don't understand much about cause
      and effect in a manufacturing enterprise. But
      that's what I wrote this book about. If you'll
      share a little of your valuable time with me, we
      can discuss the <u>real</u> problems and some of the
      tools for addressing them.

Chapter 1
Why the Excitement About MRP II Today?

Exec   We've been exploding bills of material for years and doing "requirements planning," why all the excitement about material requirements planning - MRP - today?

OW   Because what was "requirements planning" developed into the tools to make valid <u>schedules</u>. Something we never had before! And once we solved the scheduling problem, we were able to have a company game plan that worked! A set of tools to enable management to control cash flow, inventories, labor and material purchases. Tools to support marketing better and provide far more useful financial information. Tools that enable companies to reduce inventories, improve customer service, and improve overall productivity.

Exec   But wait a minute. Wasn't MRP originally an inventory control technique?

OW   MRP, or as it was called, "requirements planning," was originally used as an <u>ordering</u> technique. One company I know, for example, calculated their material requirements through the bills of material once a month, four months into the future. Each month they would add a new month, but they <u>didn't recalculate the requirements</u> for months 1, 2, and 3. In fact, the books on inventory management, back in those days, said inventory management is concerned with "When to order," and "How much to order." Before the computer came along, ordering was all the inventory control people could do. They "order launched." When the computer came along, we used it to mechanize the ordering. It didn't occur to us to use it to do something completely different that couldn't be done before.

Exec   I've heard production and inventory control called a "push system and a pull system."

OW   That expresses it well. The <u>formal</u> inventory control system pushed orders into the plant and out to the vendors. This was true whether they used order point systems or requirements planning systems, the two basic methods for determining "When to order." But the original dates on the orders were bound to be wrong before long. Back in those days, we said: "If only we could have a forecast that is correct!", "If only the engineers wouldn't make changes!", "If only the machines wouldn't break down!" We tried to get the world to hold still, but the world of manufacturing wouldn't. It was a world of change, and the original dates that were placed on orders were soon wrong. That's where the "pull system" - the informal system - came into play. It was the shortage list generated from true demand; assembly requirements in a company making an assembled product, for example.

Exec   So the pull system became the real schedule, didn't it? Why couldn't we have used it without a push system?

OW   The problem was one of lead time. The lead time for planning. When we pull parts out of a stockroom, for example, to find out what the shortages are going to be, we're faced with a dilemma: if we pull them to meet the next three weeks' assembly requirements, for example, that doesn't tell us far enough in advance what the shortages are going to be; but if we pull them to cover the next six weeks' assembly requirements, we really don't know which parts we need first. The farther out we try to extend the horizon of the shortage list, the less we know what the true priority is.

Exec   Does MRP eliminate the push/pull system?

OW   It formalizes the pull system and eliminates the push system. MRP simulates the shortage list week by week (or day by day) and recalculates requirements weekly or daily by exception messages. The shortage list says: "What are we going to make, what does it take to make it, what do we have in inventory, what do we have to get?" With the material requirements plan, we put a master production schedule into the computer (what are we going to make), we put a bill of material into the computer (what does it take to make it), we put an inventory record into the computer (what do we have), and we generate material requirements (what do we have to get). MRP is a simulator that can push the planning horizon out as far into the future as we like, yet break the time increments for planning down fine enough so that we know what the relative priority of each item really is. And it can redo the simulation weekly, or even daily.

Exec   Why did it take so long to develop MRP? We've had commercially practical computers since the mid 50's, yet even today I understand that the companies that are really using MRP well are in the minority.

OW   We were learning to use tools we never had before. We were doing things we couldn't do before. By definition, then, we didn't know what these things were. It took a lot of time and experience on the part of the users to learn how to do it. The computer made it possible to do time phasing - breaking requirements down into finer time increments - as it became more powerful and had more file space economically available. About 1961, we started recognizing that rescheduling of material already on order was at least as important as knowing "when to order." By 1971, we recognized that the master production schedule (I'll call it "master schedule" for brevity) that drove the entire MRP system was the real key to simulating the shortage lists and having schedules that represented the real needs. But this was all user developed and all from trial and error.

Exec   That's interesting because I can't remember reading much about the master schedule before the early 70's. I don't believe I ever saw an example of a master schedule until a few years back.

OW   Right. In fact, a standard format for the master schedule is something that's come about only in the last four or five years. This standard format shows what the forecast demand is, what the actual demand is, what the master build schedule is, and what items in the master schedule are still

"available to promise" in a make-to-order situation. The available to promise is uncommitted
material and capacity available for incoming customer orders. Managing the master schedule is
one of the most critical elements in making MRP
work.

Exec   You talked about rescheduling material currently
on order. Do you mean rescheduling material to
a later date as well as moving it to an earlier
date, i.e. expediting it?

OW   Absolutely. And this is an important message to
get to people who have lived in order launching
and expediting mode. The attitude often is,
"Just because one component was scrapped and
won't be in until three weeks later, I'm not about
to take the pressure off the other components.
I'll show them needed at the original due date,
rather than reschedule. If I didn't, you can be
sure that when the missing component came in I'd
be missing something else!" In a world where
schedules didn't mean very much, this attitude is
understandable. Unfortunately, it's also self-
defeating. You can't get material that you don't
need without getting it instead of material that
you do need.

The general manager of one company was ready to
fire his purchasing agent because every time they
went to make products, one or more purchased
components were missing. But the problem wasn't
really the fact that the purchasing agent wasn't
putting in the effort. The fact of the matter was
that the purchasing agent didn't know which of
the "past due" items were really needed most and
which ones to concentrate on getting in. There
were many components that were past due that
weren't needed, and a few that were past due
that were needed. The first step was to give the
purchasing agent a valid schedule so that he
knew what was really needed.

Of course, the expeditor is only looking for the
material that is needed. He sees that it is past
due and blames purchasing for not having the
material "in on time," not recognizing that there
are plenty of other items that are past due that

aren't really needed now. One of the most in-sidious by-products of the informal system is that it makes everyone's performance look bad, and everybody blames everybody else when things don't go right - which is most of the time!

Exec   Lately I've heard about "Closed Loop MRP." Just what is that?

OW   Once again, this was something that evolved from the application of material requirements planning in the real world. The elements of a Closed Loop MRP system are shown in Figure 1.

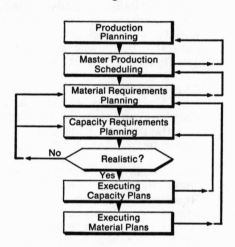

Figure 1. Closed Loop Diagram

It rapidly became obvious that the material re-quirements plan offered a powerful scheduling - or "priority planning" - capability. This is the "heart" of the closed loop system. But the ma-terial requirements plan had to be driven by a master schedule that identified the finished units in a make-to-stock business or the building blocks of assemblies or groups of components in a make-to-order business that were actually going to be made. This, in turn, was derived from the production plan which is a statement of the pro-duction rate (usually in units for a product family) like: "We are going to build 1500 'model thirty' pumps per week."

It became apparent too that if we couldn't plan the capacity requirements to meet the material requirements, the plan wasn't really valid. Here again, the fundamental manufacturing equation, "What are we going to make, what does it take to make it, what do we have, what do we have to get," is used, only this time it's in standard hours rather than units. Once the material and capacity requirements plans to execute a given production plan and master schedule have been developed, the question is whether or not these plans are realistic - are they "doable?" If they are, then the execution of the material plan will be done using a daily schedule going out to each work center on the factory floor and usually a weekly schedule going out to each vendor. The capacity plan will be executed by monitoring to see if actual output is meeting the plan.

Exec   Okay, so that's what people mean by "closing the loop." Putting in the other elements that are required to plan production and inventories in a manufacturing business. What's this MRP II we've been hearing about just recently?

OW   Once again, it was the users who took the tools they had and extended them. Manufacturing Resource Planning (MRP II) is a game plan for planning and monitoring all of the resources of a manufacturing company; manufacturing, marketing, finance, and engineering. Technically, it involves using the closed loop MRP system to generate the financial figures. Figure 2, for example, shows a regular material requirements planning format expressed in dollars. This is the pump component inventory plan derived from the material requirements plan. The first figure in the projected available balance row, 540,000, is the summary of the "on hand" inventory of components expressed in dollars taken from the material requirements plan. The requirements are also costed out, the scheduled receipts and planned orders (lumped together under "scheduled receipts" in the figure) are costed out, and a projected component inventory balance is calculated. This is the right level of stores inventory to have to support the current production rate for these pumps. If the master schedule is correct, it's a valid plan and actual performance can be monitored against it. A valid purchase commitment report (as opposed to the ones that are derived from order launching and expediting with a huge "bubble" of past due material) can be developed. Manufactured items can be broken out of the plan, and converted to capacity requirements in standard hours by work center. These can be costed out to show the amount of labor as well as the amount of material that needs to be purchased to meet a given plan. That was the first step in developing MRP II. Instead of having one set of numbers for the operating system in manufacturing and another set kept by the financial people, once the manufacturing people have numbers that are valid, the financial people can use these to get their numbers. Of course, whenever there are two systems, the numbers are bound to be different. With MRP II, everybody can be working to the same set of numbers.

Pump Component Inventory — In $(000)

		Month			
		1	2	3	4
Projected Gross Requirements		250	250	300	300
Scheduled Receipts		250	250	270	290
Proj. Avail. Bal.	540	540	540	510	500

Figure 2. Pump Component

But that's only the technical difference. The big difference comes in the way management uses these tools now that the operating plans can be translated into the common denominator of business: dollars.

MRP II is literally a simulation of a manufacturing business. It can be used to schedule the factory, schedule vendors, plan manpower far better, plan capacity requirements for new equipment more accurately farther into the future and with more capability of testing various plans. It can be used to generate the planned shipping dollars, it can be tied in with the business plan, and it can be used to simulate "what ifs" like: "What if we have to get this product out on a rush basis in 30 days, what extra capacity will be needed, what other jobs might have to be pushed aside?", "What if marketing really sells what they are saying in that new product line, will we be able to support their sales projection with material and capacity?", "What if we introduce all those new products at once, how much additional inventory will we require?" In short, Manufacturing Resource Planning becomes a company game plan for manufacturing, marketing, engineering, and finance.

Exec   It sure sounds like MRP II can do some powerful things.

OW   You're right, but that's the wrong way to say it. MRP II is just a set of tools that enables management to run a manufacturing business far more professionally. The system itself is just a simple set of logical techniques that the massive data manipulation capability of the computer has made practical. What people have learned to do with it is its real power. In the past, for example, there was usually an adversary relationship between manufacturing, marketing, engineering, and finance. They didn't have a common game plan, and they typically didn't work together as a team as well as they should have. Now we can have that game plan. Now it's up to management to use the game plan and develop an environment where teamwork is the norm rather than the exception. Americans are very individualistic - "one man, one vote." Our toughest competitors, the Japanese, are great team players. They play well together even when there isn't a game plan. We need the game plan, we've got it now. It isn't "miracle requirements planning," but it is the missing link.

Exec   I guess one thing still bothers me. Why did you call it "Manufacturing Resource Planning"? Many people are still going to think of it as something that applies only to manufacturing.

OW   That was a toughie. We could have called it something new, but I think the world is getting tired of three letter words and acronyms. It's about time we settled things down and showed management that we have a standard set of tools on the operations side of the business, just as the financial people have standard costs, budgets, cash flow, etc. Manufacturing Resource Planning did develop out of material requirements planning and that's still the scheduling guts of the system. And scheduling is fundamental in running a manufacturing business. Fundamental not just to manufacturing, but fundamental to finance (cash flow is built around timing), fundamental to marketing (customer delivery performance is built around timing), fundamental to engineering (without schedules in engineering, new product introduction, engineering change, and the delivery of highly engineered products simply won't take place on time, and the rest of the planning in a manufacturing business won't work well). Some people prefer to call it things like "Management Resource Planning" or "Business Requirements Planning," but this is not planning that applies to a theatrical agency or a real estate business, it applies to a manufacturing business. Perhaps our biggest problem is that we often fail to recognize that our businesses are manufacturing businesses; not that manufacturing is more important than marketing, engineering, and finance, but that all of the resources in a manufacturing business must be planned and coordinated properly if we're to get the best results.

Exec   It sounds like this has dramatic potential. Why don't we hear more about it? Certainly, there are occasional articles, but you would think that all of the business publications would be doing everything possible to accelerate the adoption of MRP II.

OW   Any new technology takes 20 to 30 years to really sink in. The airplane was invented in 1903, commercial airlines became a success a long, long time later. We have a new industrial revolution going on today. An ability to run a manufacturing business far more professionally. An ability very much akin to the quantum leap in professionalism that came in flying with the development of instruments. Running a business with MRP II is like flying by instrument. It gives the managers far more capability than they ever had before. But when we are in the midst of a revolution, it's difficult to see what's happening because we are too close to it. I'm sure not too many managers during the first industrial revolution said to their wives, "Skip breakfast this morning, honey. I don't want to be late for the industrial revolution." When the most dramatic things are taking place, we are usually too close to the day-to-day activity to recognize their significance. Nevertheless, we have some powerful tools available today, and if we are going to regain our position as the leader in manufacturing in the world, it behooves us to get these tools adopted and used effectively as quickly as possible.

Chapter 2
Does MRP II Apply to *My* Business?

Exec   We have a large corporation with many divisions. Are you implying that MRP will apply to <u>all</u> of these divisions? For example, we have one division making machine tools. They have a large backlog of customer orders that usually extends 18 months or more into the future. We don't make-to-forecast and it doesn't seem to me that the problems of change that MRP addresses are really part of that business.

OW   There is no question that when you have a firm backlog of customer orders, you have the best available "forecast." And it's interesting that people are always complaining about poor forecasts, yet in the typical company as their backlog of orders goes up, their <u>inventory</u> goes up too! That would seem to indicate that having a valid forecast isn't the solution to the problems of scheduling. Of course, in practice, most companies' order backlogs jiggle around like a bowl of jelly. But there are many other changes that have nothing to do with the forecast. Machines that break down, tooling that breaks, processes that go awry (there probably isn't a major manufacturing company in the country where there isn't some process - like chrome plating - that's a little marginal today, even though it worked well until last night on the four to twelve shift!). There are engineering changes, key people who are absent, vendor material that gets rejected, vendors that deliver late, and carriers who temporarily lose material. Manufacturing is a world of <u>change</u> and schedules, as a consequence, have to change or they won't reflect true need dates.

Exec   What about a company making a highly engineered product? Does it apply there?

OW   That's a very common question because people making a highly engineered product typically see MRP as a better way to order material, and ordering material isn't one of their biggest problems as long as they can get the documentation from engineering on time. But, consider a company making extruders. They had one order that was three months late because the drive unit hadn't been <u>designed</u> yet! The plant manager said, "If I got the prints and documentation tomorrow, it would be another three months before we could ship that order." Another order was one month past due for lack of an electric motor from Westinghouse; yet there was a Westinghouse motor sitting in the pile of parts that had been set aside for the job that was three months past due! The motors were very similar, although not identical. But if MRP had been used properly, Westinghouse would have been notified to reschedule the motor for the job held up for lack of the drive unit to a later need date, and they could have worked on the motor for the job that actually needed it. They actually worked on the <u>oldest</u> order first, and since the motor that wasn't needed showed an earlier due date (since it was three months past due, rather than one month past due) they sent the wrong motor to the customer - in good faith. The customer, by failing to reschedule properly, kept the job that was one month past due from being shipped. Even though a company makes a highly engineered product, their need for reschedules to keep up with the constant change is as bad as, or worse than, other kinds of manufacturing companies. And MRP II can also help with bidding, order promising, capacity planning, financial planning, and the "what if" questions.

Exec   But, frequently, engineering itself holds up manufacturing. They don't get the information to them on time.

OW   Material requirements planning is a network planning technique. It is similar to PERT (Project Evaluation and Review Technique), PMS (Project Management System), and CPM (Critical Path Method). They are all network scheduling techniques, but MRP is the simplest one. Some companies today use the same program they use for material requirements planning to plan activities for their engineering resources - the system doesn't know that a number represents an activity rather than a part! This way they have one common, simple system that they use for planning engineering as well as manufacturing. The downfall of sophisticated systems like PERT was that they were used once or twice for the original planning, but they were never kept up to date because they were not straightforward, simple, and understandable to the users.

Exec   What about our wire and cable plant? It's hard for me to visualize how MRP would apply there.

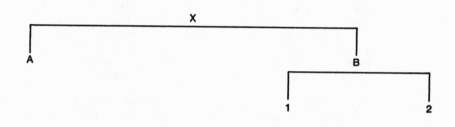

Figure 3. The Assembled Product

OW   Figure 3 shows the bill of material schematic for a company making an assembled product. X is the assembly, A and B are subassemblies, and subassembly B is made up of parts 1 and 2. Wire and cable has an upside down bill of material, like that shown in Figure 4.

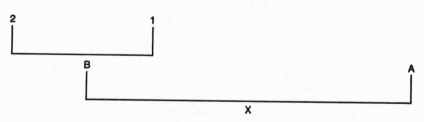

Figure 4. The Upside Down Bill of Material

Rod is extruded into wire. The wire can be tinned, or not tinned. Then it can be stranded to different numbers of strands, and it can then be given types of extruded covering, at which point the wires go to a cabler which is an assembly operation with a "right-side-up" bill of material. The upside down bill of material applies in many situations. A steel mill, for example, takes ingots and makes them into billets, rolls them into sheets, slits them into strips, rolls them down to finished size, and once again has scheduling problems; but they are not the classical fabrication and assembly type problems even though they are just as complex. One company makes forged rings that are later made into gears, etc. One forging blank in rough form can be made into several different forgings that are carried in their inventory, and others that are made to customer specifications. Once again, they have an upside down bill of material.

Exec   But what about a foundry where the material planning is usually simple? Does it apply there?

OW   I've been addressing the application of material requirements planning in your previous questions. One of the reasons that there is a lot of confusion over the application of MRP is that we think of the material scheduling only. Think of the closed loop schematic shown in Figure 1 once again. Certainly, a foundry must have a production plan, and a master schedule. Planning material requirements may well be very straightforward. In some foundries, it could be done with a pencil on the back of an envelope. (In others, cores are often a holdup, and the maintenance and repair of core boxes is a problem - cores could be scheduled with MRP very effectively.) But certainly a foundry needs to do capacity requirements planning; it has to have some kind of scheduling in the shop, and some kind of monitoring of capacity. The closed loop system applies to any kind of manufacturing business imaginable, even if the material requirements planning part of it isn't critical. And I would call it closed loop MRP even if the business was so simple that all of this planning - and replanning - could be done manually. If one were to sit down and invent a way to plan activities in a manufacturing business, there is no way to escape the closed loop logic.

Exec   We have one consumer products division where the manufacturing cost is very low. When the cost of labor - and even material - is a small percentage of the sales dollar, would MRP offer much payoff?

OW   Let's think in terms of MRP II, the company game plan. In the cosmetics business, for example, the coordination of all of the activities in the business is one of the toughest problems of all. If a major advertising campaign to promote a new fragrance takes place before the fragrance is available at the retailer, most of the advertising expenditure was a waste of money. Two or three weeks later, the lady who is a potential customer will have forgotten the name of the fragrance. And here we have a real education job to do because scheduling isn't considered to be a real important issue in a cosmetics company. But it is when manufacturing, marketing, design, advertising and procurement each work to informal, ill-coordinated plans. And that's what MRP II is all about: making valid plans so that all of the functions of a manufacturing business can work together more effectively.

Exec   What about distribution? Isn't that really more of a pure inventory management problem?

OW   Too many people think that distribution is a "different" situation when it really isn't. The traditional tools of "inventory management" and distribution were: order point, economic order quantity, and "allocation algorithms." These have been around since the late 50's, but their track record is rather poor. It would be hard to point to companies today that are saying that they have accomplished a great deal using this kind of system, even though practically every seminar or textbook on distribution inventory management mentions these techniques as the standard "tools of the trade."

Consider this example: Imagine three branch warehouses, or distribution centers (DC) as they are usually called today, that carry the same item and at each DC the inventory is just barely above order point. At the main plant warehouse, there is a back-up inventory, and it's just barely above order point. Obviously, when these three warehouses break order point almost simultaneously, there will need to be a rush replenishment order placed at the main plant. On the other hand, consider a situation where each of the DCs has just received a resupply, but the main plant is just below order point, and a replenishment order is created that probably won't be needed for some time to come. The classical order point system didn't address timing. Using MRP in distribution (we call it DRP - Distribution Resource Planning - because today it is being tied in with the financial, the traffic, the warehouse systems, and manufacturing planning) the forecast will be extended in time periods - typically weeks - into the future. Planned order releases will be created for each of the DCs and these will become the requirements against the main plant inventory. As demand changes, these requirements will change and messages indicating necessary reschedules will be generated. The DRP approach emphasizes timing, scheduling, and, in practice, it has proved to be a breakthrough in handling distribution inventories.

Some companies make their own distribution inventories and very few of them coordinate the distribution activities and the manufacturing activities well. By using the DRP approach, they will be far better off in terms of inventory investment, plant efficiency, and customer service. Other companies simply purchase and resell material. By using the DRP approach, they can show their suppliers their requirements much farther into the future, keep their requirements up to date so that they represent their real, current needs, and extend these requirements out beyond the vendors' lead times so that as vendors change lead times, they won't need to respond to these changes.

Exec   It sounds like we're talking about each of our divisions using the same system. That alone could be a great advantage to management if everybody was talking the same language.

OW   Yes, we have clients who feel very strongly about that. One I can think of has seven plants in the United States, and they all use the same kind of planning and monitoring system. Even their Mexican and overseas plants all talk the same "MRP language."

Exec   Okay, Ollie, I've got one needle for you. Back in the 60's, everybody talked about order point - you included. In the 70's and 80's, we're talking about MRP, what comes next?

OW   That's a good question! Another question that is similar to that is, "I've heard about the MRP system, what are the other choices?" The answer to both questions is the same. We finally learned how to develop a formal system that simulates the fundamental manufacturing equation that was always used in the informal system: "What are we going to make, what does it take to make it, what have we got, what have we got to get." Any system that simulates that equation is, by definition, MRP. Any system that <u>doesn't</u> will be supplemented by an informal system that <u>does</u> simulate that equation. What are the alternatives? <u>To use MRP or have the shortage list be the real schedule</u>. What comes after MRP? Well, we can call it what we will in the future, but unless we somehow figure out a way to change the fundamental manufacturing equation, it's going to look an awful lot like MRP!

Chapter 3
What Results Can We Expect?

Exec   I've heard of some rather dramatic results in companies that are using MRP well. Where do I look for these results?

OW   The results translate into one basic word - PRODUCTIVITY. Let me first summarize the kinds of results people get and then we'll talk about each of these in more detail:

1. Reduced inventory.
2. Improved customer service.
3. Improved direct labor productivity.
4. Reduced purchased cost.
5. Reduced traffic costs.
6. Reduced obsolescence.
7. Reduced overtime.
8. Having the numbers to run the business.
9. Having accountability throughout the organization.
10. Improved quality of life.

Exec   Well, I've read plenty on productivity today - you have to be hiding in a cave to miss all of the literature that addresses that subject - but I rarely read anything about MRP II and productivity. Why is that if MRP II is so good?

OW   I read the articles on productivity myself, and I truly question how many of them were ever written by anybody who knows much about what really goes on in a manufacturing business. Virtually everybody assumes that manufacturing businesses run the way they should run, and that simply isn't true. They assume that the formal scheduling system works, <u>and nothing could be farther from the truth</u>! Unfortunately, there's a lot of flailing around in addressing the productivity problem. Most of the discussions come from people who don't understand the problem and, consequently, don't understand the solution.

Exec   Well, let's talk about inventory reduction. With the cost of money today and the fact that money is often difficult to borrow at any price, that's becoming very critical in our company.

OW Making more of the right things at the right time can result in an inventory reduction. The typical MRP user - and I mean one that is doing it reasonably well, not one that has just generated paper from a computer - will get a 1/4 to 1/3 reduction in inventory investment. This translates directly into the productivity of money. When this money can be freed up, it can be used to invest in more efficient machinery, and other tools to improve productivity.

Exec I know how to reduce inventory - if I insist on a reduction, it will happen! I'm really kidding, Ollie, because I know, as well as you, that inventory reduction by edict will soon show up in poor customer service. Some of my people say that when we reduce inventory we dip into our safety stock, so we're bound to hurt customer service.

OW That was the old thinking in the order point inventory model: "Lead time is fixed and known, and the more safety stock the better the customer service." A "model" isn't a model if it doesn't represent the real world - and in the real world, lead time is highly variable - depending a great deal on how much we expedite. In the real world, no one tried to get something into stock on the due date if they knew there was a safety stock - and the more safety stock, the less they believed the schedules. MRP emphasizes scheduling - and better scheduling can result in reduced inventory and improved service.

I can't think of any good MRP user that hasn't improved customer service dramatically. One company making laboratory instruments went from 52 percent to 90 percent on time delivery, and they believe they can hit over 95 percent very soon. Think what this means in terms of the productivity of the marketing efforts! Think what it means in terms of the productivity of sales people who can go out and get new orders rather than spend their time apologizing for the fact that the last order wasn't shipped on time.

Consider service parts, a real concern for the customer who is concerned with the productivity of <u>his</u> equipment. Many companies that don't schedule well put other companies into the business of supplying parts for their products - and then call them "pirates"! The tragedy of this is that service parts usually have a very high markup. Handled well, service parts can make a disproportionate contribution to the profit picture.

Exec   You keep talking about productivity - does MRP II really have all that much impact on the productivity of direct labor?

OW   You bet. Of course, it varies substantially from company to company. The highest potential comes from the assembly area because that's the one that suffers the most from part shortages. Twenty to 40 percent improvement in productivity in assembly is not at all unusual. In the supplying operations, 5 to 10 percent improvement in productivity is about average because there is less expediting, fewer break-ins to setups, more of the right material available at the right time, etc. After an MRP system has been on the air for a while, there are even greater improvements in productivity. The bulk of the typical foreman's time today is spent expediting material, looking for material, in shortage meetings, getting product out the door with a big "push" at the end of the month, recovering from the end-of-the-month "push," moving people around on short notice to cover problems that have occurred, etc. Most companies estimate that between 60 and 80 percent of the average foreman's time is spent trying to get the job done in spite of poor schedules. The foreman's job description says, "Manage your people, direct your people, educate your people, install better methods, make sure the tooling is right, make sure the quality is right." MRP II users have proven that when foremen have time to do their jobs, productivity can improve substantially.

Exec   What about purchased costs? That seems to be a tough one because we have so little real control over our vendors.

OW Just because purchased cost is "on the other side of the wall" doesn't mean it's beyond control. Read the magazines and articles on purchasing. They talk about value analysis, better negotiation, better sourcing to reduce cost, working with engineering to standardize product and reduce cost, having yearly contracts, "blanket orders and releases" with vendors; but purchasing people don't have time to do all of these things well. And whenever they set up release rates with the vendors, the release rates are rapidly out of synchronization with actual production requirements. Purchasing people spend 60 to 80 percent of their time on expediting and paperwork such as purchase orders, requisitions, and reschedules. With an MRP system, the purchase order as such does not exist. There is a yearly letter of agreement, and a weekly computer-generated schedule that goes to the vendor. Since there are no purchase orders for productive material, no requisitions, and no reschedules (these are built right into the vendor's schedule) far less time is spent on paperwork. Since need dates are valid in a well managed MRP system, far less time is spent on expediting. This gives purchasing people more time to do the things that can reduce purchased costs.

Exec What kind of reduction in purchased costs should the typical company look for?

OW The national average runs about five percent, and that's a lot of money when you figure that most manufacturing companies spend about three dollars on purchased material for every dollar they spend on direct labor. A 5 percent reduction in purchased costs is like a 15 percent improvement in the productivity of direct labor. One company with MRP, for example, held their material cost increases to 2 percent in a year when inflation went up 11 percent. But this is highly dependent on the kind of business. A cigarette manufacturer using huge volumes of tobacco and paper, for example, is not likely to be able to reduce purchased costs through better scheduling. On the other hand, a manufacturer of machine tools that purchases a great deal of raw material components and subassemblies has an excellent opportunity to do this.

Exec   Purchasing claims that much of our air freight would be unnecessary with better scheduling.

OW   The American automobile industry in 1979 spent over 100 million dollars on premium air freight. That figure probably doesn't include the amount of money their vendors spent on premium air freight, nor does it include the cost of their own airplanes. Much of this additional traffic cost was due to poor scheduling. They can't afford to have line shortages, but their scheduling isn't that good in the short term. And any time we add cost to a product without increasing value, we are reducing productivity. Other companies spend a great deal of money on premium air freight delivering their product to their customers because their scheduling isn't good. Once again, this has a direct impact on productivity because this cost will have to be passed on to the customer sooner or later.

Exec   We have some hi-tech divisions where obsolescence, your next topic, really is hurting. But it seems to me that obsolescence "comes with the territory" in this type of business.

OW   Change "comes with the territory" - and that's what MRP is geared to. The biggest single cause of obsolescence is uncontrolled engineering change. And without good scheduling, the planning and coordination of engineering change is not going to take place as effectively as it should. Many engineering changes require using up existing supplies of components. Sometimes these components have to be used up in matched sets, and the timing of the engineering change must be planned and monitored closely because things will change in the manufacturing environment. Other companies make products like pharmaceuticals that have a shelf life. Once again, MRP, with its emphasis on timing, can be used to reduce - notice I didn't say "eliminate" - obsolescence in this kind of industry.

Exec   It isn't too hard to imagine how MRP can help to reduce overtime; and that is not only expensive. We are also finding that our workers don't like to work overtime like they used to. They want the time off.

OW   In addition to the informal scheduling system we talked about, there also was an informal capacity planning system. MRP replaces the informal system - the shortage list - with a formal scheduling system. In the same way, the informal capacity planning system that responded to problems after they happened, for the most part, can be replaced with a system that simulates what will happen in the future. Because of this enhanced planning capability, it's not unusual to see companies that have reduced their overtime to one tenth of what it was before they had MRP. This translates directly into more productivity per labor dollar. But there is more to the overtime problem than most people recognize. Anyone who has run a manufacturing company soon realizes that chronic overtime is very nonproductive. When people work more than three or four Saturdays in a row in a manufacturing company, their output starts to fall off due to fatigue and the fact that they start taking other days off the following week to make up for the leisure time they have missed. This means that the company is paying for six days of work (not to mention the overtime premium) while getting only five days' work. One manufacturing company that used to work three shifts seven days a week was able, through the better planning of materials and capacity, to get more output working three shifts five days per week after they installed MRP.

Exec   I'm particularly interested in the comments you made earlier about "getting the numbers to run the business." I find it difficult, however, to make a connection between better scheduling and our financial controls.

OW   Well, consider the "purchased commitment" report. It is made up by costing out the open purchased orders and adding them up by time periods. Because order launching and expediting generated a large "phoney backlog," there was always a big bubble of past due material. But all of the material past due and due in the first month never did show up in any one month. If that amount of material ever did come in, the company would have been in great financial trouble, and they probably wouldn't have had room to store the material! Because the operating system didn't work, the financial numbers didn't work; then the financial people had to develop fudge factors and, in fact, had no plan to compare against to determine whether the amount of material on order was correct even if they <u>did</u> believe it. Once we have an MRP II <u>system</u> operating, the financial figures are derived from the operating figures. In a manufacturing business, until the numbers work well in manufacturing, it's going to be difficult to make them work well many other places. But once they do, the accounting system can get its numbers from the manufacturing numbers. A great many companies today, for example, cycle count their inventory. This is a sampling technique, a quality control type technique for measuring performance. This cycle counting is usually done on a daily basis. If inventory records are accurate, they can be certified by an auditing firm; and there will be no need for the annual physical inventory - one of the <u>least productive</u> efforts that most manufacturing companies get involved in. Once again, if the manufacturing numbers are right, they can be used to generate the accounting numbers.

Exec   Another comment you made that intrigues me is this comment about accountability. My experience is that true accountability throughout the organization is easy to talk about, but tough to make stick in the real world.

OW   In a typical manufacturing company, accountability only exists at the top. Since accountability implies measurement, measurement requires a valid plan. We can measure the general manager on whether or not we hit the shipping budget, but we sure can't measure the assembly foreman on whether he did his job when he didn't have the parts. We can't measure the machine shop foreman on whether he did his job when his schedule wasn't valid. We can't measure the purchasing people on whether they did their job when their schedule wasn't valid. And we can't measure the scheduling people on whether they did their job properly when, in most companies, management didn't even provide them with the tools to make valid schedules! With MRP II, we _can_ make valid plans, we _can_ measure performance. And accountability to meet a plan _can_ exist throughout the organization.

Exec   Quality of life is something we're all talking about today. Job enrichment. But isn't the hassle kind of "built in" to a manufacturing business - especially if you demand high performance?

OW   Once people can start working together to a game plan they all understand, there's a lot less adversary relationship, a great deal more satisfaction when the product is going out the door, and people can see the results of the efforts that they are making. Imagine how a foreman who has just hit his schedule 100 percent - and that's not unusual with MRP - feels when he goes home at night. Imagine how a manufacturing vice president who has just hit his quarterly objectives, and is also being complimented by the marketing people, feels when he goes home at night. Imagine how anyone in a company that is able to see the results for their efforts feels, especially when most of their experience has been with the frustration of the informal system. As one manufacturing vice president said, "It certainly is a treat to be right instead of always being wrong!"

Exec   The results you talk about are so good that they're hardly credible. Are you talking potential or reality?

OW   Reality. Every bit of it can be documented. And if you really understand the problems in manufacturing and think about it, it isn't too surprising. With the informal system, we simply couldn't schedule properly. Not just in the factory, we couldn't coordinate our activities in the entire organization. Scheduling is fundamental to the effective operation of a manufacturing enterprise; and that's what MRP II is all about. It's fascinating how we love to get involved in the exotic and the esoteric, yet time and again, when we get right down to the real problems, they revolve around doing the fundamentals exceedingly well. And manufacturing companies are no exception to _that_ rule.

Chapter 4
What Does MRP II Cost?

Exec   Well, the benefits of MRP sound great, but what about the costs?

OW   The costs fall into three basic categories: Technical, Data, and People. Let's break these out.

In the TECHNICAL area we have:

1.   The cost of hardware. Most companies today have a computer. Installing an MRP system may require some additional costs for more capacity, typically file capacity, like extra disc drives or terminals.

2.   The cost of software. These are the computer programs for doing MRP. That would include the capacity planning, dispatching, financial reporting, etc. required for MRP II.

3.   The cost of systems and data processing people assigned to the project.

In the DATA area we have:

1.   The master schedule.
2.   Work centers.
3.   Cost figures.

These typically don't involve a lot of preparation for MRP.

4.   Bills of material.
5.   Inventories.
6.   Routings.

These do and they can be quite costly. They will be discussed below.

In the PEOPLE area we have:

1.   Education, both at live classes and using video courses.

2. Professional guidance from a qualified consultant.

Exec   How do you estimate the hardware costs?

OW   If you don't have a computer, you've got to get
        some computer resources that can handle the
        number of components and the number of levels in
        the bill of material that you have for your prod-
        uct. Some companies can operate with a computer
        that costs as little as $50,000 a year to lease;
        others spend as much as $50,000 per month. It's
        largely a function of the number of components,
        the complexity of the bill of material, the length
        of the planning horizon, etc. And you don't
        really need to own your own hardware. It can be
        done by teleprocessing, using a corporate com-
        puter or using a service bureau computer; or it
        can be done by a service bureau in a batch
        processing mode. Today, the costs of the hard-
        ware are down very dramatically and they will
        continue to improve in price/performance in the
        future. It's important to recognize in the hard-
        ware area that there are some one-time costs,
        especially if the hardware is being purchased;
        and some recurring costs that would occur if the
        hardware was being leased.

Exec   What about the cost of the software?

OW   Here again, prices vary all over the lot from
        about $15,000 a year for software from the com-
        puter suppliers themselves, to a $300,000 one-time
        price and $30,000 a year to maintain a sophisti-
        cated system from a software house. Often some
        of the more expensive software will require less
        work to make it usable. In many cases, however,
        the additional cost is just for "features" that
        frequently turn out to be bells and whistles that
        don't have any great, practical value. It's im-
        portant to select software carefully and, in our
        reference section at the back of the book, we tell
        you more about how to do that. Practically every
        software package you can get will need some
        modification to make it usable, not because it
        needs to be tailored to your business so much as
        the fact that it needs to be made into usable
        MRP. That's indicative of the adolescence of the

software field today, especially where manufacturing applications are concerned.

Exec   What about the cost of systems and programming
people? How many are likely to be required?
Obviously, here we're going to have a one-time as
well as a recurring cost as you discussed above.

OW   It's very difficult to pin this figure down because it can range from one or two systems and
programming people in a small company where
there aren't many programs to interface with, to
much greater numbers in a corporate environment
where many interfaces are required. Many companies are able to install an MRP system with
three or four computer systems and programming
people. It's important to avoid overwhelming the
project with people. One large corporation has
one hundred people working on their MRP project - mostly systems and programming people. I
give them little hope for ever achieving anything
because they are so overstaffed that they are
bound to become a debating "committee," not at
all action-oriented. We had an Executive Conference where we invited six chief executives
from six successful MRP users to tell us about
the results they got and what they would have
done over. One of the questions from the audi-
ence was, "How many extra people did you actually add?" Only one company added extra
people - two people - and they were both in the
stores area. They had no real out-of-pocket
costs for systems and programming people because
they simply used the ones they had and applied
them to the MRP project. Some companies even
then would allocate the cost to the project and
that's certainly their prerogative.

Exec   I'm surprised at the small numbers of people
you're talking about. I hear you recommending
that we run lean and hard. I've heard corpor-
ations talk about twenty to thirty people assigned
to the project, but you say that's not the right
way to go?

OW   I doubt that you have heard those kinds of numbers from the successes.

Exec   What about fixing bills of material?

OW   This includes correcting them and restructuring them to make sure they represent the way the products must be planned and scheduled in many cases. Our experience says that this may take in the range of two to six man years (two men one year, three men two years, etc.). We have seen companies that had to allocate even more people to the job.

Exec   What about the cost of correcting routings?

OW   That generally turns out to be somewhat less than the cost of correcting bills of material. It might be one to four man years. Remember, of course, I'm quoting average kinds of figures that could be very different from one company to another. I just want to give you some kind of a bench mark. I know companies where bills of material and routings were both so good that they had practically no work to do to get them corrected in preparing for MRP. Those companies are the exception, however.

Exec   What about the cost of correcting inventory records? I'm not sure I'm clear where these costs actually are incurred.

OW   I'm not surprised because it isn't something as simple as taking an extra "physical inventory" to correct the records. Companies typically have taken physicals at least once a year in the past, and none of them eliminated the problems so there's no reason to believe that another physical will! The real problem is in assigning accountability for transaction integrity, and that requires limited access stores. No person will accept the responsibility for making sure transactions take place as material moves without limited access stores. This doesn't necessarily mean "locked stockrooms." It does mean that there is someone at the door of the stockroom so that only authorized people can go in and out. It does mean that if material is stored in the yard area because it's extremely bulky, the yard becomes a limited access storage area even though it doesn't have a roof. The real cost of inventory record integrity comes in factories that weren't designed to have good physical control of material. The typical airplane manufacturer, automobile manufacturer, truck manufacturer, etc. usually has an assembly line sneaking down through the middle of an enormous wall-to-wall stockroom; and they have all of the short term scheduling problems that go with lack of inventory record integrity. Some companies have had to spend as much as $400,000 to re-layout their plant to give them control over stores. One school bus company that did this has found that it was an excellent investment because now they can get the right material to the right place at the right time because they have the numbers they can use to run an effective MRP system. If the numbers aren't right, MRP can only multiply them and extend them into more wrong numbers. It never corrects them. Accurate inventories weren't particularly significant in the days of the shortage list. With MRP, they are essential.

Exec   What about the cost of education and how do we do that?

OW   Live education classes are one of the indispensable ways to educate some key people. This will usually range from 5 to 10 percent of the total population of the company. In a small company with a couple of hundred people, it would probably be wise to send 20 people to live classes. In a company with 2,000 people, 100 people might be adequate. The percentage is lower in the larger company, based on the experience of our clients.

Exec   But I've heard that we have to educate practically everyone in the company. Certainly that can't all be done through live classes.

OW   That's right. The way to get to the rest of the group is through video courses. The people who have attended the live classes should now be accountable for educating their people using the video courses. That doesn't mean that they have to spend a lot of time in each video class. It does mean that they need to make sure that their people are there and that they attend, at least, the discussion sessions to be sure that their people understand what they are learning. These people, in turn, have to educate their people. It is a kind of a chain letter approach with line accountability for education - and I emphasize that. The personnel department, for example, can be a great help; but they cannot be held accountable - line management must be.

Exec   What about continuing education?

OW   Video courses should continue to be used. Some key people should be sent back to live classes after several years. And there is also an executive conference available for people to use as a means of getting an update.

Exec   Ollie, I'm sure you can take another needle! I do notice that when it comes to selecting software, one of your companies provides a service to help us do that. When it comes to live education, you have two companies that will do that. When we need video courses, we can go to another one of your companies for that. And you also supply the books that we will require. It certainly seems like an interesting coincidence!

OW   You're jibe is a good one. But it certainly is no coincidence. In 1968, after 13 years in manufacturing, and 3 years experience in educating executives on manufacturing applications at IBM where I was Manager of Industry Education for Manufacturing, I decided to leave to get into professional education. My associates told me that I was crazy to leave IBM! The consultants that I knew said that no consultant had ever really made money at education. But I felt that this was what was needed from my observations of the few successes and the many frustrating failures of the computer that I had seen in manufacturing companies. When I started making video courses in 1971, once again it was with a great deal of trepidation. Everybody said, "You're cutting your own throat. Who will come to your live classes?", but I felt that massive education was badly needed, and that this was the only solution no matter what the consequences. (Luckily, they turned out well!) To make a long story short, each of our activities was started to address a particular problem like education, software selection, etc. The only reason we publish our own books is that it cuts the lead time from manuscript to publication by about 12 months. I never wanted to be in the book publishing business and I'm still not crazy about it. But our business is helping people to be successful with MRP II - and we'll do just about anything required to accomplish that.

Exec   What about in-plant education done by an outside consultant? I've noticed that you don't have a company to do that.

OW   You're right, and that's called "putting your money where your mouth is!" I don't believe that that's an effective method. It isn't as good as live classes because it doesn't get people outside of their company where they can really open their minds. It tends to reinforce the "we're unique, we're different" approach. It lacks the peer confirmation of being with people from other companies. And it tends to be a one-shot deal. It isn't as good as video either. Certainly, one of your general foremen - who's attended a live class and is teaching his people using video - is going to have a lot more credibility with his people than some outside consultant. I've not seen the approach where the outside expert comes in for a few days to give everybody "smart pills" really work. That's why we don't use it.

Exec   What should we think about, then, for costs of education?

OW   For live classes, once you've figured out how many people you want to attend, you should estimate about $2,000 per person, including tuition, hotel expense, meals, travel expense, etc. Remember, when you're counting the number of people coming to class, one individual may get counted twice. One person might go to one of the live MRP classes and also go to one of the bill of material classes described in the reference section. The video library leases for between 10 and 18 thousand dollars a year, depending primarily on the number of people to be educated. With the video libraries we supply, there is a tailored education program made by a professional education consultant spelling out who should attend what courses, the content of the courses for each group of people in your company, what tapes should be used in each session, etc. There is more information on the video courses in the reference section.

Exec   What about professional guidance. Do you supply a consulting service?

OW   Virtually every company will need some outside consulting help to implement MRP II successfully from what we've observed. A good consultant will, in my opinion, be the "catalyst," coming in about one day every 4 to 6 weeks for the duration of the project. Plan on about 15 visits at a cost for travel, fees, etc. of approximately $2,000 per visit. To answer your question, we don't have much capacity to do consulting ourselves, but we have associates - who run their own consulting businesses - who could supply this service. People we can endorse.

Exec   Okay, we've talked about payout and we've talked about costs, and it's obvious that we'd have to get most of these numbers together for ourselves. What do you typically see in terms of payout from an MRP project in total dollars?

OW   In every one of our live classes, as well as working with clients, I do a sample justification using an actual company in the room, and using numbers supplied by people from that company. The worst justification I can recall gave an 80 percent annual return on the cost of installing MRP. In other words, if the cost was $600,000, the annual return was $480,000. And that's a recurring return. Once money is taken out of inventory, the inventory interest cost (we don't use inventory "carrying cost," just interest cost in the justification) will come back every year as long as the inventory is operated at a lower level. The best justification I can remember at the moment was a 1200 percent annual return. In other words, if the system was going to cost approximately $600,000 to install, the annual return was $7,200,000 per year recurring. The average payback runs about three to one.

There is, of course, cash flow to be kept in mind. The typical MRP system takes about 18 months to install, and it's all negative cash flow during that period. The kind of return that we're talking about should come back within the first full year that MRP II is on the air if it is installed and managed properly.

Chapter 5
Why Should the *Executive* Care?

Exec   I hear much ado about top management "support" and "involvement" if MRP is going to succeed. I'm not sure I understand why this is so necessary.

OW   I don't think either of those words really conveys the point. "Support" without understanding is a liability. And management surely doesn't need to spend a lot of time and get terribly "involved" in the nitty gritty of MRP like determining lot sizing rules. What's required is management leadership to install and operate it properly.

Exec   I still don't see why the executive has to be so involved - sorry - "provide leadership" to make a scheduling system work.

OW   But MRP II, Manufacturing Resource Planning, is not just a better scheduling system. A formal scheduling system that really works becomes the cornerstone of a real company game plan. It's a set of tools to run a business more professionally.

But to make it happen, there must be a new set of values, a new set of objectives. Inventory records have to be correct. The CEO will have to establish line accountability for meeting this objective. The bill of material can no longer just be a document that's of value to engineering and only used for reference by other parts of the company. It now becomes a control document. The master schedule can no longer be a "wish list." It has to be realistic. Top management, in some companies that have an MRP system, still believes in overstating the master schedule. This gives the same kind of results that order launching and expediting did. Many items are past due that aren't really needed. It doesn't take people very long to figure out that the system isn't telling them what they really need and they quietly revert to the shortage list.

Exec   That's an interesting thought. We really didn't tell the truth in the past, did we?

OW   No, we typically used the master schedule, for example, as "motivational information" rather than operational information. Production control put dates on purchase orders that were early because they didn't believe that purchasing would deliver on time. Purchasing didn't try to meet the dates because they knew that the dates were wrong. MRP is a system that can enable us to deal with facts to tell the truth. But that's not what our experience has been in manufacturing. And top management has got to set the example.

Exec   Okay, I understand all that, and I'm ready to do that. But I hear you saying that I've got to do even more. Like what?

OW   Well, consider implementation. In a company where head count has to be reduced due to a drop off in business, if top management doesn't understand what the MRP project is, you can be sure that the people who will be layed off will be the people fixing the bills of material, doing the cycle counting, etc. The only companies I've ever seen that lived through a head count reduction and still kept their MRP implementation project going were those where top management really understood how essential these tools are to enable them to manage the business more professionally.

Exec   Alright, what about after implementation? Where does top management come in then?

OW   I gave a talk to five hundred people recently. Approximately three hundred of them were MRP users. I asked, "How many of you have a master scheduling policy that specifies that marketing and manufacturing must get together to review the master schedule at least monthly, and then it must be signed off on by the CEO?" Less than ten people raised their hands! Isn't that incredible? The master schedule is made so that manufacturing can produce what the customers need. Yet, the people who are representing the customers often look upon MRP as just some production control system that doesn't involve them because management never explained it properly to them. At that same meeting I asked, "How many of you have a production plan that is made monthly at a meeting with marketing, manufacturing, finance, and engineering, presided over by the CEO?" Approximately six people raised their hands! Here we have the most powerful tools ever available for taking management policy and plans and translating them into detailed plans for the entire organization. Yet, in the typical company using this kind of system, <u>management doesn't formally make the plans or make the policy</u>!

Exec   It's funny, isn't it, how we looked at MRP II as some kind of a computer system. It really is a set of tools that gives us some powerful controls on the business, isn't it?

OW   Yes. And another reason why management needs to understand is that they must set the example in using the system to manage. When it's time for inventory reduction, the top manager who doesn't understand MRP will start to sign all the requisitions for over five hundred dollars. The requisitions he cancels will come back to him regularly because until such time as the master schedule is changed, the computer will continue to generate them. The real handle on inventory reduction is the master schedule. The professional top executive won't ask to sign the requisitions, but instead will call in the master scheduler, marketing, and manufacturing to see what can be taken out of the master schedule to reduce inventory. When a hot order comes in, the top executive who doesn't understand the new tools will, undoubtedly, have it hand carried through the factory and "let the chips fall where they may." The top manager who understands the tools will give it to the master scheduler and say: "Get this hand carried through the factory, but tell me and tell marketing what's going to suffer in order to get this out." The top manager who understands what the MRP tools are will use them to help in preparing the capital budget, in planning inventory levels, and cash flow. The top manager who doesn't will continue to use a separate set of numbers, and then wonder why what actually happens never coincides with the business plans.

Exec   When you say top management, how far up are you going? Should we try to talk to the chairman of the board and even the board of directors?

OW   Yes. I've seen companies where they went to a lot of trouble and expense to install MRP. Then the board of directors and the chairman hired a new president for a division - one with no real MRP II experience - who destroyed it all overnight. The minute there was a problem, he insisted on looking at the shortage lists and rolling up his sleeves and chasing shortages. Believe me. I didn't make that example up; I've seen it. It's tragic.

Exec   Getting into MRP makes me feel almost like I'm getting married.

OW   Not a bad comparison. Once you've operated with MRP your life will never be the same. We talked about the paybacks from MRP and talked about specifics. When I asked them at Xerox what they really felt they got from MRP that was of the greatest value, they said: "control" - the ability to control their dynamic, growing business. Manufacturing Resource Planning is a way to run a manufacturing business at a higher level of professionalism than we ever could before. The responsibility for running the business more professionally rests with management; and if they don't understand the new tools, they can't be expected to use them most effectively, or to set the example for other people in using the tools and placing a high priority on keeping the numbers correct.

Chapter 6
What Must Be Done To Be Successful With MRP II?

Exec   I keep hearing that there has been a low success rate with MRP. Many have tried it, but only a small percentage have really succeeded.

OW   The truth of the matter is that so far a fairly small number - probably under 200 - have managed to become Class A or B MRP users. Class A companies use MRP II as a company game plan and can get along without a shortage list because they schedule so well. The B companies have a good closed loop MRP system - good "manufacturing control" - but don't really use it as a company game plan yet. The C companies use it primarily as an inventory control system. And the D companies have it working only in data processing. Even the C companies usually get an inventory reduction. The average inventory reduction from using MRP comes out to about one-third, according to a survey quoted in Business Week, June 4, 1979. This survey taken by Professors John Anderson and Roger Schroeder at the University of Minnesota included 326 companies. At that time, there weren't many Class A and B users in the United States, so it had to include many Class C users. Average delivery performance improved from 64 percent to 81 percent, and there were many other improvements from MRP. The real issue is that most MRP users fall far short of its potential, not that they fail. The miracle is that there aren't more disasters from MRP considering the way that the typical company blunders into it. To a great extent, success has been the biggest enemy of MRP. People hear what can be done using these tools and they rush headlong into it without the faintest notion of what they're doing.

Exec   What are the mistakes people make?

OW   They often pick a data processing person as the project leader. That ignores the issue of accountability; only a user can be accountable for making the tools produce results. They get very concerned about the software. This is like a golfer who has never played spending the first six months picking golf clubs, rather than learning about the game. Most software today is quite usable, and it isn't the software that makes the difference between success and failure in most installations. (Unless the software is so bad that it simply doesn't work - and that doesn't happen often today, thank goodness.) Because people think of MRP as a computer system, they make it sophisticated. They try to put the bells and whistles into the system hoping that this will make things work better, rather than recognizing that the system should be simple so that people understand what it means and can use the information confidently and effectively.

The way management approves of expenditures is a dead giveaway to their priorities. They've already got the computer in most companies, and they're spending a lot of money on it. They sign off on the expenditure for more software. They know that things that involve the computer cost a lot of money. When it comes to signing off on an appropriation for re-layout of the plant in order to have good physical control of stores, management is considerably less enthusiastic. When it comes to spending money for education, they tend to think of that as one of those nice luxuries we do every once in a while to kind of boost the morale of the people, rather than recognizing that it is a prerequisite to intelligent use of the better tools. Their priorities are exactly backwards! They should give education the highest priority on the plan, data integrity next, and software lowest. Not that they don't have to have software to do MRP. It must use standard MRP logic and it must work. But some of the best MRP installations in the country today use some of the most rudimentary software programs available.

Exec   I was interested in your comment about people having to make things work. We sure lost sight of that in the early days of the computer.

OW   Unfortunately, not everybody has learned from the school of hard knocks, but the people who are doing it successfully today learned the lessons and learned them well. The amateurs are waiting for the tools to actually do the job. But no computer ever added capacity, for example. Capacity is added by people who know what the numbers generated by the computer mean. These people, not the computer, will decide whether to work overtime, add manpower, buy more machinery, subcontract, use alternate routings, etc.

Exec   But why is it so different? What makes it so easy to take the wrong turn so frequently in developing an MRP system? From what I've heard, most people, given a choice, will make the wrong decision.

OW   There are really two basic reasons:

1. They perceive MRP to be a computer system rather than a people system made possible by the computer.
2. They fail to recognize that the major challenge will be for a lot of people to make the transition from the informal system environment to a formal system.

Running a manufacturing business with a formal system that works is simply not an extension of our experience. In the past, overstated master schedules were used regularly to "motivate the troops." Inventory record accuracy, for example, was not particularly important in the world of the shortage list. Even today, I hear of controllers who "don't believe in cycle counting." That's like a pilot who "doesn't believe in altimeters" - how else can inventory record accuracy be measured continuously? Today, there is a body of knowledge. There is a set of standard tools available to the professional. But we've got a lot to do to get everybody to understand.

Exec   Can you summarize for me then, Ollie, what must be done to make MRP work?

OW   Yes. It all boils down to approaching this as a people system:

1. In the technical area, use a standard system. Don't fall for the old line "we're unique, we're different." The fundamental

manufacturing equation applies to every manufacturing business I've ever seen, and I've been in over 1300 factories in the last 30 years and talked with thousands of executives. That doesn't necessarily mean that you have to use a purchased software program. You can write your own, but you must use standard logic. And don't let your people get the "computer virus" and complicate things. If people don't understand the logic of a system, they will not know why it told them to do what it did. Their choices are to obey it blindly or ignore it completely. Simplicity is a prerequisite to understanding. Understanding is a prerequisite to accountability. We have to teach people that the ultimate sophistication is simplicity.

2.   In the data area, the most critical items are the bills of material, routings, and inventory records. (Work center identification, cost figures, and the master schedule are not usually areas that require major development efforts.) Inventory record accuracy will require:

   a.   Setting that as an objective.

   b.   Establishing line accountability from the top right down to the stores manager for inventory record accuracy.

   c.   Measuring performance - using cycle counting, a daily sampling of the inventory records.

   d.   Correcting the problems.

3.   The people area mainly revolves around education.

Everybody in the company should have some degree of education before MRP really goes on the air. Before the pilot goes on the air, 70 to 80 percent of the total population of the company should have some degree of education. Machine operators at the most

successful companies get an hour of education each month, usually using about a
half hour of video tape and a half hour of
discussion with their foreman and perhaps
some other member of management.

While everybody needs to be educated, two
groups require particular attention: top
management and first-line supervision like
foremen. We talked about top management's
role, and many people understand that
today. But many people fail to recognize
that real control will come from execution.
And the execution of better schedules has to
take place through the line organization.
The foremen are the people who have to
make it happen. They've usually heard
about computer systems before, and they've
usually seen few that produced anything but
more paper, more work, and more frustration. MRP is simple. It's a way to predict
the shortages farther into the future so that
the foremen can be working this month to
prevent next month's problems, rather than
finding out about them one week before they
happen. But if they don't understand MRP,
and if they don't put as much effort into
preventing problems as they do today into
fixing problems after they happen, MRP will
never attain its real potential.

Lastly, I would emphasize that education
itself is not a fact transfer. That's why we
don't recommend bringing in the outside
expert to do the job. That's why there are
so few educators who really have a track
record of successful clients. There's never
been a successful MRP installation without
some torchbearers. If the educators can't
convey an enthusiasm for running the business more professionally, MRP simply won't
happen. How, for example, does a company
manage to operate, get shipments out the
door, and tackle a project as ambitious as
MRP? Obviously, they can't - and I told
you earlier that they don't - add a lot of
extra people. Temporary help isn't going to
be very useful in fixing bills of material, for

example. This has to be done with their own people. It means a lot of hard work from dedicated, enthusiastic people. And if education doesn't convey that enthusiasm, it is worthless.

Exec   What's the best environment for installing MRP? Is it a function of a company's size, its product, the complexity of its business, or what?

OW   Today, MRP can be applied economically in companies doing 2 million or more in sales because of the low cost of some of the computer hardware and software that is available. Frankly, it's easier to install MRP in a small company because there are fewer people to educate, fewer people who have to change the way they live. But large companies, like Xerox, have done it. It required a massive education program. The biggest problem with some large companies is that they tend to be very inbred and don't look outside to see what's going on because they "know" that they are doing it the best possible way. The automobile companies, for example, tend to suffer from a great deal of "intellectual incest" because they believe they are unique and different when, in fact, they aren't.

As for the product, that has practically nothing to do with it. The more complex the product, the more complex the scheduling problems, the more necessary it is to have MRP; but that doesn't mean that it's going to be a good environment for installing it. The environment really boils down to people and management. I look for a company where they have stability in the management. I saw one company where 80 percent of the top executives were new within a nine-month period. Most of the new managers were concerned primarily with short term objectives. They were afraid they wouldn't be there for another twelve months if they didn't get ahead on the political side very, very quickly. That is not a good environment for installing MRP.

I look for a company that is very people-oriented. Somehow MRP seems to fit very well into a company like that because it is basically a set of tools to help people do their jobs better. I look for a company where they understand fundamentals of management like how to establish objectives and accountability even before they have MRP. Once they have the more powerful tools, a company like this will be able to get a lot better results than a company that doesn't know how to manage well.

MRP is certainly not a substitute for management in any way. The best environment for successful MRP is a well-managed company. Professionals, given better tools to work with, can get unbelievable results. At the Chair Plant of Steelcase, where they produce over 20,000 chairs a week, 2,000 customer orders, they have been on schedule 233 out of 234 consecutive weeks. (If I had told them that was possible when they were implementing MRP, they would have laughed at me!) At the Cameron Iron Works plant in Leeds, England, they are getting excellent results from MRP and their plant manager said to their executive vice president, "Ollie Wight is a lousy salesman. When you do it well, it's a lot better than he describes it." At Abbott Laboratories in Canada, they wrote an article in which they understandably bragged about the fact that they were hitting their master schedule 96 percent of the time. By the time the article got published, they had hit it 100 percent for three consecutive weeks. The results in a well-managed company will be beyond their expectations, from my experience.

Chapter 7
How Do We Implement MRP II?

Exec   You've told us <u>what</u> has to be done.   Now let's talk about <u>how</u> to do it.   How do we implement it?

OW   There are six basic steps in implementation:

1.   The first-cut education.
2.   The justification.
3.   Picking a full time project leader.
4.   Professional guidance.
5.   Making up a project plan and establishing accountability for the elements in that plan.
6.   A regular management review.

Exec   Who would be involved in that first-cut education?

OW   The purpose of the first-cut education is to prepare some key people to do a justification, so only a few people should be involved.   We recommend sending the following to the Top Management Class:

1.   Chief Executive Officer (General Manager or President usually).
2.   Vice President of Manufacturing.
3.   Vice President of Finance.
4.   Vice President of Engineering.
5.   Vice President of Marketing.
6.   Vice President of Administration.
7.   Vice President of Human Resources.

Then we recommend sending the following people - primarily their counterparts one level down - to the five-day class (all of these classes are described in the reference section at the back of the book):

1.   Plant Manager.
2.   Materials Manager.
3.   Purchasing Manager.
4.   Accounting Manager.

5. Engineering Manager.
6. Marketing Manager.
7. Systems Manager.
8. Personnel Manager.

Exec   You've told us about results and costs, do you have any hints on handling the justification?

OW   Well, as I mentioned, we use the cost of money in looking at the return on an inventory reduction. If two million dollars is estimated to be the potential inventory reduction, we would probably use a number like 15 percent, assuming that the cost of money will vary between 10 and 20 percent over the next few years. That would amount to $300,000 a year. For customer service, we normally look at what additional business - not due to increased normal growth - due to better customer service would be anticipated. If sales were expected to increase by 2 million dollars, for example, then 10 percent of that, or $200,000, would be the number that we would usually use as a pretax return. This, again, is conservative for most companies, especially since it represents incremental business. Productivity is usually estimated by figuring the number of people in assembly and subassembly areas, multiplying that by the costs to keep them on the payroll (salary plus out-of-pocket fringes, etc.) and attaching a percentage figure to that. Nonassembly areas are usually calculated separately because they represent a smaller percentage of productivity improvement. We don't usually put anything in for the productivity improvement to be anticipated from having more of the foreman's time available to do his job. But management should recognize that the potential exists and should set high expectations for improved cost reduction, etc. because the foreman does have that time available when the firefighting is dramatically reduced. The purchased material savings area is pretty straightforward. The return is typically about 5 percent of the total purchased cost in companies where more time available to the people can result in cost reductions. I don't think there are any other particular hints to give you in the area of costs that haven't already been covered.

Exec   Okay, what about this project leader?

OW   This is one of the classic places where people seem to be magnetically attracted to making the wrong turn. There are four major mistakes that I've seen made:

1.   Picking a data processing or systems person as project leader. This violates that principle of accountability.

2.   Hiring an MRP "expert" from outside of the company to be the project leader. Not that a person like this couldn't be part of the project team, but it's much easier to teach a person who knows your company, your products, and your people about MRP than it is to teach an MRP "expert" about your company, your products, and your people. Take one of your own people who has a high level of credibility within the company and a good deal of experience.

3.   Picking a "lightweight." One company picked a young man just out of college to be the project leader. He was a fine person with plenty of potential, but his credibility with the people, like first-line supervision, was nonexistent. Once again, management saw MRP as a computer system and assigned him to the project because he had a degree in computer science!

4.   Making the job of installing MRP a part-time project for the project leader. Unfortunately, the day-to-day firefighting will always take precedence and it will take forever to install a system.

Exec   Ollie, you sound pretty hard-nosed about the right and wrong way to go about this.

OW   I know what works. You're playing a game that includes both odds and stakes. The stakes are very high. While few companies "fail" with MRP in terms of having a real disaster, most companies need the results and most CEOs will be measured on achieving them. What do they do for an encore? The problems won't go away or get easier. They've already got people who are skeptical, and some who are even cynical about anything that even smacks of the computer. If they don't make it as Class A or B this time, it'll be a long time before they get another chance. The stakes are simply too high to take any chances. The odds can be made just about 100 percent for success. There's a way to do it right. It's been proven. People who take the short cuts are exposing themselves to risks that appear reasonable only to the inexperienced.

Exec   What about the area of professional guidance? We talked about the cost of consulting before, but how can we be sure we are getting a competent consultant? Most of us have had the experience of hiring a consultant who left us with a lot of flow charts and notebooks, but not much else.

OW   This certainly is an area where it's easy to make a mistake. I personally don't agree with the philosophy of most large consulting firms. I think it's all wrong for the following reasons:

1.   They want to do it for you because the more people they rent out to you, the more money they make.

2.   Most of their people are technical people. Thus, their concentration is on the "system" - the least significant part of the project. Not that it doesn't have to be done right, but it's the management part of MRP that's the tough part. It's making the transition from the world of the informal system to the world of the formal system. And most consulting firms have very few people who can contribute much in this critical area.

3.   Because they make money renting bodies, they love to reinvent the wheel; this is not the way to keep a system standard and simple. Usually, the system turns out to be theirs, not yours. You'd be far better off to get their best man to come in once every four to six weeks, rather than have that

person sell you the job and "supervise it" while a bunch of inexperienced people learn at your expense.

4.   The excuse of some of these consultants is that just being the catalyst won't work for many companies because they "need more help than that." Yes, that's often true. But the help they need is not in the systems area where the consultants have the most competence, but in the management area where they, for the most part, are ill-qualified to help. Not that these consultants aren't sincere, but most of them still think that the "system" will do it. That's one of the reasons that they have such an awful track record for client success. <u>No</u> system can substitute for good management. If management isn't capable of installing MRP without a lot of "hand-holding," their chances of being able to manage with MRP after it is installed are slim indeed. The track record of consulting proves that.

It's up to you to check the consultant out. I know consultants who've written books, who give talks, and who are well known in our field. But finding their successful clients would be extremely challenging. If a consultant or educator cannot show you where they have clients who are successful as a result of the consultant's assistance, that person should not be used in your MRP project. Check their credentials. Don't believe what they tell you without talking to their clients and proving, to your own satisfaction, that they have the competence to help you.

Exec   That makes sense. What is the "project plan"?

OW   We've made a generalized implementation plan based on the experiences of companies that have installed MRP successfully. It goes into the steps of implementation like fixing inventory records, bills of material, and education in considerable detail; and it shows the sequence of the important elements in installing an MRP II system. It's included in this book after the section on references. Use it to make your own project plan.

Plagiarize it. Cross off the items that don't apply to your company, add in a few that do, if there are any. It's a road map for doing MRP successfully that's been used by a great many companies and should be a great help to your company.

Exec   Just what exactly do you mean here by "account-ability"?

OW   Every element of the project plan should have a name and a time attached to it. The person on the project team should be accountable for getting this accomplished. Some people will be on the project team full time, typically a few people from engineering, for example, who are fixing bills of material, systems people, etc. Others, like people from accounting, may only have to be participating part-time. But they should have specific assignments and be held accountable for accomplishing them. And you know whose name should be at the top of the project plan, don't you? The CEO. This isn't just another ploy to make the CEO's life tough. It's already tough. But, in the event the company spends a half a million to three-quarters of a million dollars installing an MRP system, and it doesn't produce results, you can be sure that the CEO will be held responsible. It's good to start right out with that person's name on the top of the project plan so people know that this is not another data processing exercise, but is a serious business project and that management is providing the leadership.

Exec   How often must management review the project?

OW   Every two weeks or so the management steering committee, consisting of the CEO and the top executives from each of the major functions, should review the project plan to see what is being done, what tasks are in trouble, and what needs to be done to get the project back on the track. This should be taken as seriously as if a new plant were being built. In fact, I've been through building new plants and installing MRP II and, frankly, MRP II is more challenging. Not that it can't be done, but it cannot be approached cavalierly as a computer project if you expect to get results.

Exec   I'm a little nervous about how we convert to a new system like MRP II without totally upsetting the company and running the risk of getting into serious trouble, at least at the very beginning. How do we accomplish this?

OW   There are three fundamental ways of converting to MRP:

1.   The "cold turkey" approach says, "Pull the big switch Monday, and put MRP II on the air across the board." This is irresponsible. No company should ever use this approach. Only a few companies have done it successfully, and every one of them that I talk to recommends against other companies using that approach. One company said, "It almost did us in." Other companies have been done in by the cold turkey approach. They overwhelmed their people and they never did get the results they should have from MRP.

2.   Running systems in "parallel" doesn't work for MRP because MRP is a system that couldn't be done manually. Therefore, manual systems that are now on the computer can not be used in parallel with MRP because they will produce conflicting information.

3.   The "pilot" approach is ill-understood by most people. They want to know, "What product line should we pick?" "Should it be the easiest one?" "Should it be the most difficult one?" "How will we know whether it's working in the factory when we don't have valid need dates on everything, only the items in the pilot?" None of these questions are valid. The issues are to pick a person, not a product - the most enthusiastic, hard-working planner in the company, the one that is most likely to make MRP work. Then check to make sure that he understands the system and is able to operate without a shortage list. That means

the material requirements planning pilot is
working.

Exec   How do we know whether we're ready to go on
the air with the MRP pilot or not?

OW   Inventory records should be 95 percent accurate
using cycle counting as a measure. Cycle
counting is done daily on a sample group of
items. If 100 items are counted, and 95 out of
100 percent are within a reasonable counting
tolerance, that is 95 percent inventory record
accuracy. Experience shows that without this
level of accuracy, data integrity will be a real
problem in making MRP work. Ninety-eight to 99
percent of the bills of material should be 100
percent accurate. Ninety-five to 98 percent of
the routings should be 100 percent accurate.
Seventy-five to 80 percent of the people should
have at least some degree of education before the
pilot is even started with 100 percent of the
people as a final goal These are the most
critical areas.

Exec   What's a reasonable time schedule for installing
MRP?

OW   I like to see my clients put the pilot material
requirements planning system on the air in nine
to twelve months. I like to see them have all of
material requirements planning on the air in
another three months. All of capacity planning,
shop floor control, vendor scheduling, and accounting should be working in another three
months. That's a fifteen to eighteen month
period of time.

Exec   Wow! That's an ambitious schedule. How can a
project this big be accomplished that fast?

OW   In Chapter 4 and Chapter 6, we discussed the
technical, data, and people areas that need to be
handled to make MRP work. The time-consuming
elements of an MRP system are:

1.   Technical - development and implementation
of the software and systems.

2. <u>Data</u> - bills of material, inventory records, and routings.

3. <u>People</u> - education.

These are the items in the critical path. If it looks like MRP is going to take more than eighteen months, they should be reviewed to see what can be done to shorten up the time.

Exec   Why are you so adamant about doing this on such a tight time schedule?

OW   There are two very good reasons. If you take an extra year to install MRP and the system has been justified based on an annual savings of one million dollars a year, the extra year will cost you one million dollars that you'll never have another chance to recover. But even more important is the problem of the span of attention of people from management right on down. As I told you earlier, MRP requires dedication and especially <u>enthusiasm</u> on the part of everyone. Keeping that enthusiasm at a high peak, and running the business at the same time with all the normal problems of manufacturing like hitting schedules, customer problems, competitive problems, labor problems, government regulations from OSHA and the FDA for example, environment problems, product liability problems, etc. is tough. The odds against maintaining that level of enthusiasm for much over two years are staggering. Companies that plan MRP to take a long time and make the installation schedules nice and "comfortable" will probably still be installing MRP six years from now and aren't very likely to ever see the real success that management can achieve from these better tools.

Chapter 8
How Do We Manage With MRP II?

Exec   What's really different about managing using MRP II?

OW   With MRP II, the CEO is responsible for:

1.   Establishing objectives.

2.   Establishing accountability.

3.   <u>Making the production plan.</u>

4.   Making sure that the plan is valid, that the data is correct, that the master schedule represents what's really going to be built.

5.   Establishing policy on subjects like master scheduling.

6.   Making sure that every member of the management team uses the system rather than "end-running" it. It is a new set of tools and people will instinctively come up with excuses for not using it like, "But we needed that order out in a real hurry." In a good MRP system, there is no reason why the order can't be delivered just as quickly as it could if end-running the system, and with a lot more knowledge of what the consequences will be.

7.   Measuring performance against valid plans.

8.   Measuring people on their execution of the plans.

9.   Getting rid of the adversary relationships and getting people to work together as a team far better than was possible before.

Exec   Wait a minute. Back up here. Does the CEO really have to <u>make</u> the production plan?

OW   The production plan is a production rate for a product family usually expressed in units. Companies have many production plans for their different product families. The production plan starts by looking at current backlog for a make-to-order product or current inventory for a make-to-stock product. If the production plan was being made for one year in the future, for example, the desired change in ending backlog or inventory would be added to or subtracted from the sales forecast for the product family to determine the production rate required. Production plans are often made a year or two in advance, broken down into quarters and months, and then reviewed monthly. At the monthly meeting, the top operating executive should bring together the top marketing, manufacturing, finance, and engineering people to establish these production plans. Whether the top executive does the actual calculations is unimportant. The point is that with a closed loop MRP system and MRP II, top level planning can be translated right down to the detail level, and it's extremely important that the top level planning be done properly.

Exec   And you say this is <u>my</u> responsibility, Ollie?

OW   Absolutely. It's been said that there are three conflicting objectives in a manufacturing company: maximum customer service, minimum inventory, and maximum plant efficiency. These objectives have to be reconciled to come up with reasonable plans. These plans will determine the levels of inventory, the levels of production and, as a consequence, will determine cash flow, return on investment, etc. The tools are here now so that management can get results from better planning. But it's up to management to do that better planning. They now have a great deal more control over their own destinies.

Exec   Okay, Ollie, that's a new perspective. You know the rest of what you say doesn't really sound like anything new. It just sounds like good management. Aren't you talking about "management by objectives"?

OW   Management by objectives (MBO) to me is just common sense. I don't see anything startling about it. Perhaps that is what's so great about it. As I understand it, it all started when Peter Drucker said, "Let's spend less time worrying about what we are doing, and more time worrying about what we are trying to accomplish." I guess all good things are simple in retrospect. Yes, MRP II and MBO go hand in hand. In fact, I don't know how MBO could really work in a manufacturing environment without the valid plans that MRP II makes possible. I believe that MRP II is a prerequisite to effective MBO. One of the reasons why MBO has not produced all of the results it should have in the past was that, once again, people assumed that things worked the way they should in a factory and didn't recognize that valid plans simply didn't exist. On the other hand, now that the more professional tools are here, the "MBO" approach - if you want to call it that - <u>must</u> be used to make it really work.

Exec   Do we really have <u>different</u> objectives with MRP II than we did before?

OW   Yes, especially in the area of inventory record accuracy, bills of material, the master schedule; and now we spell out objectives and establish accountability where we really didn't before. Now we have line accountability for inventory accuracy, for example, and measure managers on performance against this objective. One company I know has a "logistics group" that reports to marketing that generates the master schedule. At first, this sounds frightening. But, in fact, the marketing group has the objectives of keeping plant employment at a level rate and providing a doable plan. As long as they have those objectives, there's no reason why marketing can't make valid plans for manufacturing. I worked in a company once where 80 percent of the business came in from branch warehouses that reported to marketing. It was a disaster. In a highly seasonal business, they virtually shut the factory down during the off season and ordered everything in sight during the peak season without accepting any responsibility for keeping the plant operating at a level rate. But that was the fault of management, not the fault of marketing. It's management's responsibility to set the proper objectives, and translate these objectives into higher level planning through the production plans. With the tools we have today, these higher level plans can be translated into valid plans right down through the organization.

Exec   The more you think about MRP II, the more sense it makes. It really is a way to eliminate a lot of today's frustration and confusion.

OW   It definitely is. Consider a company that had three assembly plants all drawing from one fabrication plant. The fabrication plant manager was always in trouble because whenever something wasn't shipped, the assembly plants could produce a shortage list that showed that the missing items were "past due" from the fabrication plant. Of course they were! With order launching and expediting, virtually everything was "past due." Another company has a working MRP system. They have a fabrication plant manager and an assembly plant manager. But their fabrication plant manager isn't constantly in trouble. He has a valid schedule. As long as he works to that schedule, the right material will be made and assembly can meet their schedule. In the world of the informal system, there was always confusing, conflicting information. In the world of MRP II, plans should make sense, they should be attainable, and if each member of the team executes his plans, the company objectives will be met.

Exec   Ollie, doesn't management have to formalize some things that weren't really spelled out before?

OW   Yes, like written policies for things like the production plan and the master schedule. These weren't particularly significant before, but now they are. Wouldn't it be interesting, for example, to have manufacturing write down their understanding of how far out the master schedule ought to be held firm and not changed, except for a real crisis, and marketing's ideas about this same kind of policy - and what constituted a real crisis! We would, undoubtedly, get a very different set of answers. And this kind of policy needs to be worked out ahead of time, answering some fundamental questions. How often must the forecast be reviewed? How often will a production planning meeting take place? Who will attend it? Who will be responsible for what input to the production plan? How will it be measured? Who will sign off on the production plan? When can changes be made in the master schedule? We need some guidelines for knowing when changes can be made quite readily and when they'll have to be checked to see if they are doable. One company, for example, makes any change within the first four weeks subject to approval by the vice president of manufacturing, any in the next four weeks by the director of materials management, and beyond that, the master scheduler can make the changes. In the past, we didn't have the tools to execute these policies in a methodical way. Now we have the tools and it's management's responsibility to get people together to spell out these policies. It's important to establish the ground rules before the ball goes into play, rather than debating the ground rules constantly after the ball is in play.

Exec   And management must set the example for keeping the numbers right?

OW   Yes. That was something that wasn't particularly important before. I sent a young man down to Black and Decker many years ago to see their MRP system. He was a very perceptive person. His reaction was, "Everything impressed me, but what impressed me the most was their immense respect for numbers." The pilot who flies by instrument has an immense respect for numbers!

Exec   You talked about some of the things we had to measure before we implemented the system, like inventory record accuracy, bills of material, and routings. How will we measure the system after it goes on the air?

OW   We will have to measure these on a continuing basis. We can measure bills of material by counting the number of times the assembly department, for example, has to go back to the stockroom to get material because of a bill of material error. If 100 bills were issued in a week and one error was reported, that's 99 percent.

Routings will be measured by feedback from the daily shop schedule that we call a "dispatch report." If a job is in the department but doesn't show on the dispatch report, or vice versa, it will have to be checked out. If this is due to a routing error and two are discovered during a week when 100 routings were issued, that's a 98 percent routing accuracy. Other elements that need to be measured are:

The master schedule. Typically, companies take a "snapshot" of it once a month and then measure what percentage of the individual items were actually made. They then find out why the items in the master schedule weren't made. Identifying the causes of the problems, and fixing them, is part of execution.

Shipping dollars. This is usually already measured in most companies today.

Delivery performance. Most companies measure this in one way or another and should continue to.

Schedules. Output in standard hours by work center should be measured against the capacity plan. Shop, vendor, and engineering orders and projects completed on schedule against the total orders promised for a given time period should be measured.

Forecasts. I'm not really terribly concerned about how forecasts are measured, as long as we measure them some way because everything that's measured tends to improve.

Of course, the essence of good control is to audit and find out what's actually causing the problems and what has to be done to improve performance. The measurement doesn't do that - it simply identifies the fact that there are problems.

One of the key measures, in my opinion, is the shortage list. The reason this is such a powerful measure is that we can use it to track down the causes of the shortages to find out why they are happening. In fact, if you are really operating

MRP II at a Class A level, there <u>should not be a shortage list</u>.

Exec   <u>No</u> shortage list? Can people really make that <u>happen</u>?

OW   Why not? MRP is just a simulation of the short-age list. If it's being used properly to prevent the shortages, there's no reason to have a short-age list. But one of the important messages for management to get across is that MRP is not going to make that happen, <u>people</u> are going to make it happen. Whatever you do, <u>don't fire your expeditor</u> when you put in MRP! Too many people get the impression that somehow we just won't have to exert the effort with MRP, and that simply isn't true. There won't be as many crises - that's for sure. But there will still be the vendor that has scrap at the last minute, the quality problem that shows up in assembly, and that's when a company will need the same kind of "can do" spirit they had before. People will have to exert the same kind of effort they do to <u>fix</u> the shortages now, and use it to <u>prevent</u> the shortages with MRP. Steelcase, for example, still flies an occasional part in. The difference is that they do it far less than ever before and they do it in order to hit the schedule 100 percent!

Exec   Okay, Ollie, you make a good point. The real results are going to come from the execution of MRP. Have MRP users learned anything about execution - making it happen - beyond just "good management"?

OW   One of the approaches that we have found to be very helpful is to list each manager's top ten problems. You know the old 80/20 rule, the vital few, and the trivial many? Identify these prob-lems, have the manager sign off on what the solutions are and when they will be accomplished, and then measure the manager's performance in solving these problems correctly and on time.

Exec   And the emphasis with MRP II is on teamwork, isn't it? Everyone has to play his position.

OW   Yes, and you know we've talked about teamwork for years to the point where many people are sick of hearing about it. But we were missing that vital link - valid plans. Plans, obviously, won't make teamwork happen; management must do that. But even the most dedicated management is going to have trouble getting real teamwork without the game plan to do it. MRP II is that game plan.

Exec   And you say if we do install MRP II properly, MRP II will work - I mean MRP will give us the tools so that we can get the results?

OW   Every time. Without fail. There is a right way to implement MRP II, and if you do it properly, it will work. You talked about the "failures" earlier. Take a look at the people who didn't succeed and look at the way they approached it. Find out who their project manager was. Where did they put the emphasis? Did they do the right education job? Inevitably, you'll find that they approached it as a computer system, not a people system. They didn't recognize that it was a new, more professional way to run a manufacturing business made possible by some tools that were made possible by the computer.

Exec   Okay, Ollie, what's your forecast for the future? How is management of a manufacturing company going to be changing as a result of these tools?

OW   I see a number of changes taking place:

1. There will be a lot more emphasis on managing a manufacturing business as a profession. This is vital not only to our economy, but to our society.

2. We will put a lot more emphasis on establishing the proper objectives and measuring performance rather than the "organization-itis" that many companies use today in the hopes of somehow "osmoting" the right objectives to the right part of the company. I don't care if the stockroom reports to the personnel department as long as the personnel manager is held accountable for getting material out to the shop floor, keeping records accurate, etc.

3. I think we've got the gee whiz days of the computer behind us. I think we've learned from the school of hard knocks not just in the MRP area, but in many other areas. Now our real emphasis has to be on <u>using</u> these tools - not as an end in themselves - but as a way to enhance our capabilities in utilizing the most important resources we have in our manufacturing industries, our <u>human resources</u>.

References
Sources for Further Information on MRP and MRP II

Section 1
The Needs

Any company installing a closed loop MRP or MRP II system will need a number of types of professional assistance. Among these are:

1. Books on the subject.

2. Education in live classes.

3. In-plant education using video courses.

4. Reviews of commercially available software packages for MRP and MRP II. Companies using their own system rather than buying software should be sure that their system has the ability to perform the proper functions for MRP and MRP II. There is a <u>standard</u> system that will work. Very few deviations from the standard can actually work in practice.

5. Consulting services to help install the system or review it periodically after it has been implemented and is operating.

The following sections indicate a number of the services that are available in this field.

Section 2
Other Available Books

1. MRP II: Unlocking America's Productivity Potential, Oliver W. Wight, published jointly by CBI Publishing Company, Boston, Massachusetts, and OWL Publications, Inc., Burlington, Vermont, 1981. This book describes MRP II as the missing link in productivity, explains the new set of values and responsibilities that management will have to use to get the potential improvements in productivity by using MRP II, describes how MRP II applies in every facet of the business including marketing, finance, engineering, data processing, etc., and then tells how to be a Class A user.

2. Production and Inventory Management in the Computer Age, Oliver W. Wight, CBI Publishing Company, Inc., Boston, MA, 1974. This book, as its name implies, covers the subject of production and inventory management in the computer age with heavy emphasis on MRP. It also covers other areas like capacity planning, shop floor control, purchasing, etc.

3. Material Requirements Planning, Joseph Orlicky, McGraw-Hill Book Company, New York, 1975. This is an excellent technical exposition of material requirements planning and that is its basic emphasis as opposed to the entire closed loop system. This would be an excellent book for a systems designer who wanted to understand the detailed logic of a material requirements planning system.

4. Master Production Scheduling; Principles and Practice, William L. Berry, Thomas E. Vollman, D. Clay Whybark, American Production and Inventory Control Society, Washington, D.C., 1979. This is an excellent review of current master production scheduling practice at some of the best MRP users in the country.

5. Focus Forecasting: Computer Techniques for Inventory Control, Bernard T. Smith, CBI Publishing Company, Inc., Boston, MA, 1978. This is a detailed explanation of the focus forecasting sys-

tem.   A number of different forecasting strategies can be used within the focus forecasting system. The system tests each of these against the most recent sales to see which works best, and then uses this strategy to forecast the immediate future.   Focus forecasting has had great success at American Hardware Supply Company where thousands of individual items of virtually every kind have to be forecast.

6.   DRP - Distribution Resource Planning,   Andre Martin, OWL Publications, Inc., Williston, Vermont, 1982.   This is a description of the way distribution requirements planning and distribution resource planning can be applied in a company with branch warehouses and distribution centers.   It is particularly valuable for those companies that have manufacturing which must be integrated with a distribution system.

7.   APICS Dictionary (Editor for 1980 edition; Thomas Wallace),   American Production and Inventory Control Society, Washington, D.C., 1980.

It is fascinating to observe the lack of books on MRP and related subjects.   There are several other books on MRP, but any books where there is little real information on MRP, or where there is a significant amount of misinformation about MRP, have been omitted.   For example, books that discuss MRP strictly as an order launching technique, don't discuss master scheduling, etc. were not listed.

Section 3
Live Classes

These are classes run by consultants who teach MRP and related subjects. No attempt has been made to include classes taught by anyone other than the education professionals involved in Oliver Wight, Inc. and Oliver Wight Education Associates. A list that would appear to be "objective" would include a number of classes that the author does not consider to be professional because of the content, or the fact that the instructors don't have a track record for MRP success. Information on other classes is available from the American Production and Inventory Control Society, P.O. Box 219, Falls Church, Virginia 22046.

MRP II: Manufacturing Resource Planning for Top Management (two and a half day class). Instructors: Walter Goddard and Oliver Wight.

MRP II: Manufacturing Resource Planning (The Five-Day Class) is taught by the following instructors:

Roger Brooks and Al Stevens (West Coast)
R. D. Garwood (Atlanta)
Walter Goddard and Oliver Wight (Boston and Florida)

Other Related Courses

Subject	Duration	Instructors
Bills of Material	3 days	Dave Garwood
Capacity Planning & Shop Floor Control	3 days	Dick Alban
Distribution Resource Planning	3 days	Andre Martin
MRP II: Financial Management	3 days	Andre Martin
Inventory Record Accuracy	2 days	Roger Brooks

Master Production Scheduling	4 days	Dick Ling (East Coast) Al Stevens (West Coast)
MRP II: Successful Implementation	3 days	George Bevis & Tom Wallace
The Planner's Job	2 days	Tom Wallace
MRP II for Purchasing	3 days	John Schorr & Tom Wallace
MRP II for Service Parts	2 days	Dave Garwood

Most of these classes are also run in the United Kingdom in conjunction with our associate, Mike Salmon. Classes - taught in French - are also scheduled regularly in France.

Further information on these classes is available from Oliver Wight Education Associates, Inc., P.O. Box 313, Newbury, NH 03255. 800-258-3862 or 603-763-2061.

Section 4
Video Education Courses

Video education is an essential tool for educating enough people to really make MRP work. It would never be practical to send enough people off to live classes. Bringing in the "outside expert" to run classes has proved to be a very nonproductive approach for reasons discussed in the text of this book.

The following courses are available from Oliver Wight Video Productions, Inc., P.O. Box 278, Williston, VT 05495:

Managing Inventories and Production by Oliver W. Wight.

Managing a Master Production Schedule by Walter E. Goddard.

MRP II: Making it Work by Walter Goddard, Darryl Landvater, and Oliver Wight.

Bills of Material by Dave Garwood.

The Key to MRP Success: A New Set of Values by Oliver Wight.

MRP II: Manufacturing Resource Planning by Oliver Wight.

MRP II: Unlocking America's Productivity Potential by Oliver Wight.

Section 5
Software Reviews

At one time, there was one computer program available from a computer manufacturer or software supplier for doing MRP. This program was the only one for many years. Today, there are over 100 different programs available and before a user gets involved with any set of programs, it would be well to know what is in the programs. Manufacturing Software Systems, P.O. Box 278, Williston, VT 05495, is the only known source for software evaluations. This is a kind of "consumer report" for software users.

The basic point of reference is a book called the "Standard System." It lists and explains the functions any MRP software must perform to operate properly. This book was developed based on the experience of successful MRP users. Available also are evaluations of the most popular computer software programs available from computer manufacturers and software suppliers. These evaluations compare the available software with the Standard System, indicating whether or not the software will perform the functions properly, and also indicating what modifications will have to be made to the software if it does not perform these functions properly.

Even a company with its own in-house computer program for MRP and MRP II would probably be well advised to get a copy of the Standard System to make sure their programs are properly designed.

Section 6
Consulting

There are many consultants who claim to have expertise in MRP. Some of them known to the author have experience, but only in seeing MRP installations fail. As MRP has become the recognized approach to running a manufacturing business more professionally, every consultant that can explain what the letters stand for is offering services in the field. There is a group of people endorsed specifically by the author, people who are involved in Oliver Wight Education Associates. (A list of endorsed consultants is available.) There <u>are</u> other consultants in the field. A list of MRP consultants is available from the American Production and Inventory Control Society (APICS, P.O. Box 219, Falls Church, Virginia 22046). Anyone engaging a consultant should <u>check the consultant's references</u> to make <u>sure</u> they have <u>current implementation experience</u>. The most successful installations have been the ones where a consultant came in once a month or once every six weeks to guide and be the catalyst rather than being on site every day, because that tends to take the initiative for developing a system away from the users.

The Implementation Plan

This implementation plan was developed by Darryl Landvater, President of Manufacturing Software Systems, Inc. It has been updated to include the financial functions that would be included in an MRP II system. In its earlier form, it has been used by hundreds of companies as a road map for implementing MRP successfully.

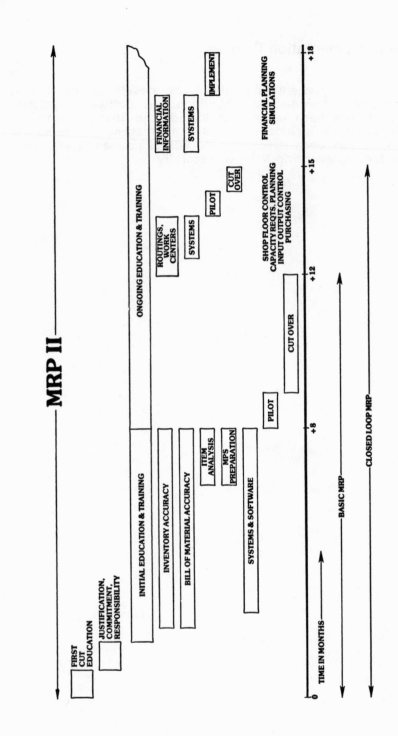

MRP II

MRP II DETAILED IMPLEMENTATION PLAN

More and more people are asking for information on the implementation and operation of MRP systems. These people are not interested in being sold on MRP. MRP systems work. The proof is available and companies are using them every day. People who understand the fundamentals and the logical simplicity of MRP are looking for a proven way to implement the system.

This detailed implementation plan is a road map to help people implement MRP systems. The implementation plan outlines the basic functional areas needed to implement MRP. These functional areas are then broken down into specific milestones. This listing of broad functional areas and specific tasks provides a very practical plan.

PEOPLE USING MRP

The implementation plan is also meant for companies using an MRP system. There are many companies which have the technical part of an MRP system in place. Yet, they are not using the system well. The implementation plan can help these companies. The jobs in improving an MRP system are the same as the jobs to implement it correctly. The only difference is that some of these jobs may have already been done. If so, they can be deleted from the plan.

MRP II

MRP, which started out over ten years ago as a better way to order material, has evolved into MRP II. MRP II is a total company-wide system. It is a way to get all the people in the company working to the same game plan; to the same set of numbers. A company can now plan material, capacity, finance, marketing strategy, etc. all with the same system. In addition, all these things can be simulated to provide the management of the company with real planning capability.

This version of the implementation plan includes the steps for MRP II.

Finally, the implementation plan has been put on video tape. The course MRP: Making It Work, available from Oliver Wight Video Productions, Inc., uses this implementation plan as the core of the section on implementing MRP. Each of the points in this implementation plan are expanded significantly and explained in that video course.

USING THE PLAN

The implementation plan is a generalized framework applicable to nearly any company. Its two primary uses are:

1. To provide a clear statement of priorities - to separate the vital and trivial, and keep them in perspective.
2. To provide a road map for implementation.

The implementation plan is organized to constantly focus attention on the items that have the greatest impact on the potential for success. The people part of an MRP system is fully 80% of the system. The system will only work when people understand what it is, how it works, and what their responsibilities are. For this reason, the education and training are listed at the front of the implementation plan. The computer software and programming effort is not as likely to be something which prevents the success of an MRP system, and so this topic is covered later in the plan.

The other purpose is to provide a detailed schedule of events that have to be accomplished in order to implement the system. The most effective way to use the plan is to tailor the plan to each company and then use it as the agenda for management reviews of implementation progress.

PRACTICALITY

This implementation plan is not a theoretical exercise. In the six years since the first version of the plan was developed, it has been used successfully by a number of companies. Whether these companies would have been successful without the plan, I cannot say. But it does work, it is practical, and those who have used it swear by it.

TAILORING THE PLAN TO YOUR COMPANY

The implementation plan is a general framework stated in terms of departments and job titles. The departments and job titles should be replaced by the names of the people within the organization who will be responsible for the tasks.

The implementation plan also contains an approximate time frame for scheduling the tasks under each of the functional topics. The scheduled due dates for the tasks in implementation are given under the heading "DATE." These due dates were developed based on the dependence of some tasks on others. The times on the plan, +3 and +7 for example, are months relative to a starting point. A time of +3 means the task should be completed three months after the start date. The start date used in the plan is the date that formal commitment is given to the project.

The plan should be rewritten to include calendar dates in place of the scheduled completion dates in months. Columns should also be added for the scheduled start date, the actual start date, and the actual completion date. The scheduled start dates are not on the generalized plan since the size of the different tasks will vary from company to company. The actual start and actual completion dates should be included on the plan to indicate the progress or lack of it during the management reviews of implementation.

The comments column on the implementation plan is meant to give a short explanation of the phases of the plan and tasks that make up each phase. Some people choose to leave these explanations in the final version of the plan, others leave them out. In either case, additional comments on the progress of the tasks should also be included as the plan is periodically updated. These comments would indicate, for example, the results of the cycle counts, or any other information about one of the items in the plan.

A company may also have to add or delete tasks from the implementation plan to account for situations that are a part of the implementation, or work that has already been done. As an example of an item that would be deleted from the plan, a company may have already enclosed the stockrooms and may have started cycle counting. In this case, it makes no sense to count 100 parts as a starting point. As an example of an item that would have to be added to the plan, a company may have to convert to a different computer to do MRP. In this case, the conversion from one computer to the other should be included on the detailed implementation plan.

Figure 1 is an example of the implementation plan before and after it has been tailored to a company. This example includes replacement of departments and job titles with people's names, the inclusion of calendar dates with columns for scheduling dates, and some comments on tasks that are working.

MRP DETAILED IMPLEMENTATION PLAN

TASK	RESPONSIBLE	DATE	COMMENTS
A. Measure 100 parts as a starting point.	Stockroom Mgr.	+1	This will help assess the work that needs to be done to bring the inventory records to 95%.
B. Map out limited access to the stockroom areas.	Stockroom Mgr.	+1	Lay out any stockroom changes that are necessary to insure limited access.
C. Provide the tools for limited access and transaction recording.	Top Management Stockroom Mgr. Team Leader DP Mgr.	+3	A fence, enough stockroom people, adequate space, counting scales, transaction forms, labels, skids, etc.

TASK	RESPONSIBLE	– SCHEDULED – START	DUE	– ACTUAL – START	DUE
A. Measure 100 parts as a starting point	R. Ferris	6/20/80	6/27/80	6/20/80	6/24/80
		Results indicate that the inventory accuracy is 63%.			
B. Map out limited access to the stockroom areas.	R. Ferris K. Miller	6/1/80	7/1/80	6/5/80	
		Lay out any stockroom changes that are necessary to insure limited access. Main and spare parts stockrooms to be enclosed and third stockroom to be consolidated into the existing stockrooms.			
C. Provide the tools for limited access and transaction recording.	D. Roser R. Ferris K. Miller H. Arner	7/15/80	9/1/80		
		A fence, enough stockroom people, adequate space, counting scales, transaction forms, labels, skids, etc.			

MRP DETAILED IMPLEMENTATION PLAN

TASK	RESPONSIBLE	DATE	COMMENTS
1. First-cut education.	Top Management P&IC Shop Management	−1	What is MRP and how does it work? Why should we as a company commit to it? The courses should be the equivalent of the following courses offered by Oliver Wight, Inc. P.O. Box 435 Newbury, New Hampshire 03255 (800) 258-3862 or (603) 763-5926
	Top Management P&IC Shop Management		MRP II: Manufacturing Resource Planning For Top Management MRP II: Manufacturing Resource Planning—5-Day
2. Justification, commitment, and assignment of responsibility.	Top Management P&IC Shop Management	0	Formal commitment to the project.
A. Prepare justification.	P&IC Shop Management	0	Cost/Benefit
B. Commit to the project.	Top Management	0	
C. Set up implementation team and team leader.	Top Management	0	Implementation team leader is full time. His responsibility is to make the MRP system work by coordinating and managing the project.
D. Schedule periodic management project reviews.	Top Management	0	Approximately every month. To include all those responsible for parts of the project currently active.
E. Schedule periodic visits from a consultant with experience in implementing successful MRP systems.	Top Management	0	The consultant should have successfully implemented a system or worked with successful systems. Schedule visits from once a month to once every three months.

TASK	RESPONSIBLE	DATE	COMMENTS
3. Detailed education and training.	Team Leader	0+8	This phase of the plan is aimed at the people part of the system.
			The objective of this part of the plan is to give the people operating the system an understanding of the system and the means to use it effectively. Education and training must translate the general principles of MRP into the specifics of operation at the company.
			The plan separates education and training. Education is the broad-based understanding of MRP which is essential. Training is the detailed knowledge of reports, forms, etc.
			The education and training are structured in levels. People in the company attend outside courses. These people then serve as teachers and train their own people.
A. Outside courses for people who will be teachers at the in-house courses.		+1+3	The courses should be the equivalent of the following courses offered by Oliver Wight, Inc. & Oliver Wight Education Associates, Inc. P.O. Box 313 Newbury, New Hampshire 03255 (800) 258-3862 or (603) 763-2061
	Team Leader		MRP II: Manufacturing Resource Planning - 5 day
	Steering Committee Chairman		MRP II: Successful Implementation
	P & IC Mgr.		MRP II: Successful Implementation
	Purch. Mgr.		MRP II: Manufacturing Resource Planning - 5 day
	Plant Supt.		MRP II: Manufacturing Resource Planning - 5 day
	Stockroom Mgr.		MRP II: Manufacturing Resource Planning - 5 day
	Engineering Mgr.		MRP II: Manufacturing Resource Planning - 5 day
			MRP II: Manufacturing Resource Planning for Top Management
	Sales/Marketing Mgr.		MRP II: Manufacturing Resource Planning for Top Management
	DP Mgr.		MRP II: Manufacturing Resource Planning - 5 day

MRP DETAILED IMPLEMENTATION PLAN

TASK	RESPONSIBLE	DATE	COMMENTS
B. Purchase or lease the MRP video courses for in-house education.	Team Leader	+1	These video courses will serve as the framework for all the educational courses in the following educational plan. The current library consists of 53 video tapes, approximately 33 hours of video-taped education on MRP.
			The MRP video library is available through: Oliver Wight Video Productions, Inc. P.O. Box 278 Williston, Vermont 05495 (802) 878-8161
C. Teachers course. Video education.	Team Leader	+ 1½	The team leader and all teachers go through the video courses to translate the general principles of MRP into the specifics of operation at the company. *Attendees:* All teachers. *Length:* Approx. 80 hrs.
D. Top Management course. Video education.	Team Leader	+2+8	*Attendees:* Pres., all VPs, Plant Superintendent, others as appropriate. *Length:* Approx. 40 hrs.
E. Production and inventory control. Video education.	P&IC Mgr.	+2+8	*Attendees:* All people in P&IC. *Length:* Approx. 80 hrs.
Outside workshop.	Master Scheduler	+3	Outside master scheduling workshop for one or more master schedulers. The workshop should be the equivalent of the one offered by Oliver Wight Education Associates, Inc.

TASK	RESPONSIBLE	DATE	COMMENTS
In-house training.	P&IC Mgr.	+7+8	*Attendees:* All people in P&IC. *Coverage:* All forms, reports, and documents that will be used by the people in P&IC. This includes a dry run of the system, sometimes called a "conference room pilot," to gain experience in using the reports and transactions.
F. Purchasing. Video education	Purch. Mgr.	+2+8	*Attendees:* All people in purchasing. *Length:* Approx. 45 hrs.
Outside workshop.	Purch. Mgr. Buyers	+5	Outside purchasing workshop for one or more buyers. The workshop should be the equivalent of the one offered by Oliver Wight Education Associates, Inc.
In-house training.	Purch. Mgr.	+7+8	*Attendees:* All people in purchasing. *Coverage:* All forms, reports, and documents that will be used by the people in purchasing. This includes a dry run of the system, sometimes called a "conference room pilot," to gain experience in using the reports and transactions.
G. Shop foreman. Video education.	VP Mfg. Plant Supt.	+2+8	*Attendees:* All shop foremen. *Length:* Approx. 40-45 hrs.
Outside workshop.	Shop Foreman	+5	Outside shop floor control and capacity requirements planning workshop. The workshop would be the equivalent of the one offered by Oliver Wight Education Associates, Inc.
In-house training.	Plant Supt.	+7+8	*Attendees:* All shop foremen. *Coverage:* All forms, reports, and documents that will be used by the shop people. This includes a dry run using the documents.

MRP DETAILED IMPLEMENTATION PLAN

TASK	RESPONSIBLE	DATE	COMMENTS
H. Stockroom people. Video education.	Stockroom Mgr.	+2+4	*Attendees:* Anyone who will be making inventory transactions. *Length:* Approx. 15 hrs.
Outside workshop.	Stockroom Mgr.	+3	Outside inventory accuracy workshop for one or more stockroom managers. The workshop should be the equivalent of the one offered by Oliver Wight Education Associates, Inc.
In-house training.	Stockroom Mgr.	+3	*Attendees:* Anyone who will be making inventory transactions. *Coverage:* All forms, reports, and documents that will be used in the inventory transaction system.
I. Sales and marketing. Video education.	Sales/Mktg. Mgr.	+3+8	*Attendees:* All sales and marketing people. This course is usually divided into two courses. One for those people in-house and one for those in district sales offices. *Length:* Approx. 25-30 hrs.
In-house training.	Sales/Mktg. Leader	+8	*Attendees:* All in-house sales and marketing people. *Coverage:* All forms, reports, and documents used in master scheduling and forecasting applicable to the sales and marketing people.

TASK	RESPONSIBLE	DATE	COMMENTS
J. Engineering. Video education.	Engr. Mgr.	+2+8	*Attendees:* Anyone who will be working with bills of material or routings. *Length:* Approx. 30-40 hrs.
Outside workshop.	Engr. Mgr.	+3	Outside bill of material structuring workshop for the engineering manager and several of the engineers who will be structuring bills of material. The bill of material workshop should be the equivalent of the workshop offered by Oliver Wight Education Associates, Inc.
In-house training.	Engr. Mgr.	+5	*Attendees:* Anyone who will be working with bills of material or routings. *Coverage:* All forms, reports, and documents that will be used to maintain bills of material and routings.
K. Data processing. Video education.	DP Mgr.	+2+8	*Attendees:* Anyone who will be working with the MRP programs or files. *Length:* Approx. 55 hrs.
L. Finance. Video education.	Mgr. Finance/ Accounting	+2+8	*Attendees:* All people in finance. *Length:* Approx. 35 hrs.
Outside workshop.	Mgr. Finance/ Accounting	+2+8	Outside finance and accounting workshop for one or more managers of finance and/or accounting. The workshop should be the equivalent of the one offered by Oliver Wight Education Associates, Inc.
M. Lead men and set-up men.	Shop Foremen	+2+8	*Attendees:* All set-up or lead men. *Length:* Approx. 20 hrs.

MRP DETAILED IMPLEMENTATION PLAN

TASK	RESPONSIBLE	DATE	COMMENTS
N. Distribution center managers. Video education.	Distribution Mgr.	+2 +8	*Attendees:* All distribution center or branch warehouse managers. *Length:* Approx. 20 hrs.
Outside workshop.	Distribution Mgr. DC Mgrs. Master Scheduler P&IC Mgr.	+3	Outside distribution resource planning workshop for the manager of distribution, one or more distribution center or branch warehouse managers, one or more master schedulers, P&IC manager. The workshop should be the equivalent of the one offered by Oliver Wight Education Associates, Inc.
O. Distribution center employees. Video education.	DC Mgrs.	+3 +8	*Attendees:* All distribution center employees. *Length:* Approx. 15 hrs.
P. Introduction to all direct labor employees.	V P Mfg. Plant Supt.	+3 +8	*Attendees:* All direct labor employees. *Length:* Approx. 2 hrs.
Q. Anyone else affected by the system and not covered in the courses above.	Team Leader	+8	*Attendees:* As required. *Length:* As required.
4. Inventory accuracy.	Stockroom Mgr.	+8	This phase of the plan is aimed at bringing the inventory accuracy to 95% of the items within the counting error. This must be accomplished before the pilot program can be started. This includes distribution centers or branch warehouses.
A. Measure 100 parts as a starting point.	Stockroom Mgr.	+1	This will help assess the work that needs to be done to bring the inventory records to 95%.
B. Map out limited access to the stockroom areas.	Stockroom Mgr.	+1	Lay out any stockroom changes that are necessary to insure limited access.

TASK	RESPONSIBLE	DATE	COMMENTS
C. Provide the tools for limited access and transaction recording.	Top Management Stockroom Mgr. Team Leader DP Mgr.	+3	A fence, enough stockroom people, adequate space, counting scales, transaction forms, labels, skids, etc.
D. Assign responsibility for the inventory accuracy.	Top Management	+3	The inventory manager and his people are now responsible for the inventory accuracy. Change job descriptions where necessary.
E. Start counting a control group of 100 parts.	Stockroom Mgr.	+3	Control group parts are counted once every ten days. Any inventory errors are investigated to find the cause of the error.
F. Each ten days a report is published showing the results of the control group.	Stockroom Mgr.	+3 on	The report should show the history of the inventory accuracy and the cause of the errors.
G. Start cycle counting all inventory items.	Stockroom Mgr.	+5 on	All parts are counted periodically. A simple method would be to count A and B items twice a year, and the C items once a year.
H. Bring the inventory accuracy to 95% of the parts within counting error.	Stockroom Mgr.	+8	As measured by the results of cycle counting the items in inventory, and not based only on the control group items.
5. Bill of material accuracy.	Engr. Mgr. P&IC Mgr.	+8	This phase of the plan is aimed at bringing bill of material accuracy to 98%. The tasks in this phase must be completed before the pilot program can begin. Both design and production engineering should participate in structuring the bills of material.

MRP DETAILED IMPLEMENTATION PLAN

TASK	RESPONSIBLE	DATE	COMMENTS
A. Measure 100 bills of material as a starting point.	Engineering	+3	This will help assess the work that needs to be done to eliminate errors from the bills of material.
B. Decide and assign responsibility for the accuracy of bills of material.	Top Management	+3	This may involve centralizing some responsibilities and setting up procedures to control the flow of documents if these are not already present.
C. Verify the bills of material for correct part numbers and quantities per assembly.	Engineering	+8	This requires either a line by line audit or an exception system, like stockroom pulls, to point out bill of material errors. Either method must highlight and correct any errors in component part numbers or quantities per assembly.
D. Verify the bills of material to show the correct structure of the product.	Engineering	+8	This requires restructuring the bills where necessary to show: 1. The way material moves on the shop floor. 2. Raw materials on the bills of material. 3. Modules or self-consumed assemblies where needed.
E. Decide on and implement bill of material policies.	Top Management Engineering P&IC	+5	Policies: 1. Engineering change procedure. 2. Documenting new or special products.
6. Item analysis.	P&IC Mgr.	+8	This phase of the plan covers the verification or assignment of the ordering rules.
A. Measure 100 items as a starting point.	P&IC Purch. Team Leader	+1	The parts are checked for correct lead times, ordering quantities, and safety stock (if applicable). This measurement will help assess the work that needs to be done.

TASK	RESPONSIBLE	DATE	COMMENTS
B. Agree upon and assign responsibility for the ordering rules.	P&IC Purch.	+2	Responsibilities depend on how purchasing fits into the organization and whether or not the planner/buyer concept is used.
C. Verify or establish ordering policies.	P&IC Purch.	+8	Decide between fixed order policy or lot-for-lot ordering. Dynamic order policies like part period balancing are not recommended.
D. Verify or establish order quantities and order modifiers.	P&IC Purch.	+8	Assign order quantities for fixed order policy items. Modifiers should be assigned where they are appropriate.
E. Verify or establish lead times.	P&IC Purch.	+8	*Manufactured parts:* 1. Use simple scheduling rules. 2. Be consistent. *Purchased parts:* 1. Use current lead times.
F. Verify or establish safety stock levels.	P&IC Purch.	+8	*Independent demand items:* 1. Consistent with the master schedule policy. *Dependent demand items:* 1. In special circumstances.
7. Master production schedule preparation.	Top Management Marketing P&IC Shop Management	+8	This phase of the plan covers the work required to set up a working master production schedule. Must include resource requirements planning.
A. Develop a production planning function.	Top Management Marketing P&IC Shop Management	+6	Production planning is basic strategic planning to develop a statement of production which is in families of products and by months.

MRP DETAILED IMPLEMENTATION PLAN

TASK	RESPONSIBLE	DATE	COMMENTS
B. Develop a master scheduling function.	P&IC	+6	Master scheduling takes the production plan and translates it into a specific statement of production. The master schedule is a statement of production in specific item numbers and by weeks.
C. Develop a master schedule policy.	Top Management Marketing P&IC Shop Management	+6	The master schedule policy should cover the following points for both production planning and master scheduling: 1. Procedure for changing the production plan or master production schedule. This procedure should include who can request a change, how the proposed change is investigated, and who should approve it before it is implemented. 2. Periodic reviews of the forecast and actual sales, also the master schedule and the actual production. The purpose of these reviews is to determine whether or not the production plan or master production schedule should be changed.
D. Begin operating the production plan and master production schedule.	Top Management Marketing P&IC Shop Management	+8	The first production plan and master production schedule are developed.

TASK	RESPONSIBLE	DATE	COMMENTS
8. Systems work and software selection.	DP Mgr.	+8	This phase of the plan outlines the work that needs to be done in selecting software and accomplishing the systems work and programming for the MRP system.
A. Review and select software to be used.	Data Processing P&IC Shop Management	+2	Software should be evaluated using the software evaluations from: Manufacturing Software Systems, Inc. P.O. Box 278 Williston, Vermont 05495 (802) 878-5254
B. Systems work, programming, and testing of inventory transactions.	Data Processing	+5	Issues, receipts, cycle counting.
C. Systems work, programming, and testing of bills of material.	Data Processing	+6	Normal bill of material functions.
D. Systems work, programming, and testing of scheduled receipts.	Data Processing	+6½	Scheduled receipts: 1. Manufacturing orders. 2. Purchase orders. 3. Distribution orders.
E. Systems work, programming, and testing of the MRP logic.	Data Processing	+8	Any modifications that need to be made.
F. Systems work, programming, and testing of the master schedule system.	Data Processing	+8	Master scheduling and production planning support.
G. Agree on time schedules and cutoff times.	Data Processing	+6	Times for reports, transactions and cutoff times for transactions to the system.

MRP DETAILED IMPLEMENTATION PLAN

TASK	RESPONSIBLE	DATE	COMMENTS
9. Pre-installation tasks.	P&IC Mgr. Team Leader	+8	This phase of the plan covers the tasks that immediately precede the pilot program. Must include some form of shop dispatching.
A. Set up planner structure and part responsibilities.	P&IC	+8	Which planners are responsible for which groups of parts? Decide among vertical or horizontal responsibility: 1. Vertical-product line oriented. 2. Horizontal-department oriented.
B. Set up procedures for handling both top down and bottom up closed loop planning.	P&IC Shop Foremen Purchasing	+8	Specific procedures for rescheduling, order release, and feedback of anticipated delays.
C. Physical clean-up.	P&IC Shop Foremen Purchasing	+8	Physical clean-up of the shop floor to insure that each open order has the required component parts, and that all parts on the floor are on an open order. Parts not covered by a shop order should be returned to the stockroom. All manufacturing orders and purchase orders should be verified.
10. Pilot program.	Everyone involved so far.	+8+9	This is the pilot program. It is a trial run of the system on one or a group of product lines that total several hundred part numbers. The purpose is to verify that the system is giving correct information.
A. Monitor the critical measurements.	Team Leader	+8+9	Verify that the system is providing correct information and that people are comfortable using the system.

TASK	RESPONSIBLE	DATE	COMMENTS
11. Cut over.	Everyone involved so far.	+9+12	This phase of the plan outlines the sequence that is used to move from the pilot program to full implementation on all product lines.
A. Group the remaining product lines into three or four divisions.	P&IC	+9	Divisions should contain product lines that are similar or share common parts.
B. Bring each division onto MRP, one division at a time.	P&IC	+9+12	As each division is put onto MRP, set up planner coverage so the product lines involved get intense planner coverage until they are quieted down.

END OF FIRST MAJOR SECTION IN IMPLEMENTATION

TASK	RESPONSIBLE	DATE	COMMENTS
12. Training for shop floor control, capacity requirements planning, input output control, and purchasing.	Shop Management	+15	This phase of the plan outlines the training for shop floor control, capacity requirements planning and purchasing. This training has the same objectives and the same basic course outline as the MRP training covered previously.
A. Shop Foremen. In-house training.	Plant Supt.	+15	*Attendees:* All shop foremen. *Coverage:* All forms, reports and documents that will be used in the shop floor control and capacity requirements planning systems.
B. Planners. In-house training.	P&IC Mgr.	+15	*Attendees:* All planners that will be working with the shop people. *Coverage:* All forms, reports, and documents that will be used in the shop floor control and capacity requirements planning systems.

MRP DETAILED IMPLEMENTATION PLAN

TASK	RESPONSIBLE	DATE	COMMENTS
C. Shop dispatchers. In-house training.	Shop foremen	+15	*Attendees:* All shop dispatchers. *Coverage:* All forms, reports and documents that will be used in the shop floor control and capacity requirements planning systems.
D. Purchasing. In-house training.	Purch. Mgr.	+15	*Attendees:* All purchasing people. *Coverage:* All forms, reports and documents that will be used in vendor follow-up and vendor negotiation.
13. Routing accuracy.	Shop Foremen Prod. Engr.	+15	This phase of the plan outlines the work that needs to be done to get routing accuracy to 95%.
A. Measure 100 routings as a starting point.	Shop Foremen Prod. Engr.	+10	This will help assess the work that needs to be done to eliminate errors from the routings.
B. Decide on and assign responsibility for the accuracy of the routings.	Top Management	+11	This may involve centralizing some responsibilities or defining areas of responsibilities if these do not already exist.
C. Verify that the routings show the operations correctly.	Shop Foremen Prod. Engr.	+15	This requires either a line by line audit of the routings or an exception system to point out routing errors. Either method must highlight and correct the errors in the routings. The routings should be verified for the following: 1. The correct operations and work centers. 2. The correct operation sequence. 3. A reasonable standard that can be used in scheduling.

TASK	RESPONSIBLE	DATE	COMMENTS
14. Work center identification.	Shop Foremen Prod. Engr.	+15	This phase of the plan outlines the simple steps that are required to define and classify the work centers.
A. Identify work centers.	Shop Foremen Prod. Engr.	+15	Decide which machines or groups of machines will be called work centers. In some cases a single machine will be a work center. In others, a group of similar machines will be a work center.
B. Establish an approximate work center capacity & desired Q.	Shop Foremen	+15	The work center capacity should be developed simply. This is typically done by using the actual output over the last month or so to give the demonstrated capacity for the work center.
15. Systems work.	DP Mgr.	+15	This phase of the plan outlines the systems work and programming that must be done for shop floor control and capacity requirements planning.
A. Systems work, programming, and testing of shop floor control.	Data Processing	+15	Shop floor control functions.
B. Systems work, programming, and testing of capacity requirements planning.	Data Processing	+15	Capacity requirements planning functions.
C. Systems work, programming, and testing of input/output control.	Data Processing	+15	Input/output control report.
D. Systems work, programming, and testing for purchasing.	Data Processing	+15	Vendor follow-up and vendor negotiation reports.

MRP DETAILED IMPLEMENTATION PLAN

TASK	RESPONSIBLE	DATE	COMMENTS
16. Implementation of shop floor control.	Shop Foremen P&IC	+ 15 + 16	The implementation of shop floor control uses a pilot program since new transactions and disciplines are being used on the shop floor.
A. Implement shop floor control on a pilot group of parts.	Shop Foremen P&IC	+ 15	The pilot should be large enough to provide one hundred or so shop orders. It is also helpful to use a product line that will create shop orders under shop floor control in all departments.
B. Implement shop floor control on the remaining items.	Shop Foremen P&IC	+ 15½	Cut over remaining items.
17. Implement capacity requirements planning, input/output control, and purchasing.	Shop Foremen P&IC Purch. Mgr.	+ 16	This is a simple implementation. Capacity requirements planning, input/output control and purchasing negotiation reports are simply stated.

END OF SECOND MAJOR SECTION IN IMPLEMENTATION

TASK	RESPONSIBLE	DATE	COMMENTS
18. Training for financial planning and simulation.	Mgr. Finance/ Accounting, P&IC Mgr.	+18	This phase of the plan outlines the training for financial planning and simulations. This training has the same objectives and the same basic course outline as the MRP training covered previously.
A. Finance and accounting. In-house training.	Mgr. Finance/ Accounting	+18	*Attendees:* People in finance and accounting. *Coverage:* All forms, reports and documents that will be used.
B. Production and inventory control. In-house training.	P&IC Mgr.	+18	*Attendees:* People in P&IC. *Coverage:* Differences between simulations and normal operation of the system.
19. Develop financial planning numbers.	Mgr. Finance/ Accounting	+18	These numbers are used to do inventory projections, cash flow projections, and fixed overhead allocations. Numbers include: 1. Cost by item. 2. Labor costs. 3. Machinery operating costs. 4. Fixed overhead allocations by work center, group of work centers, or departments.

MRP DETAILED IMPLEMENTATION PLAN

TASK	RESPONSIBLE	DATE	COMMENTS
20. Implement financial planning and simulations.	Mgr. Finance/ Accounting P&IC Mgr.	+18	No pilot is needed. Begin running the programs and verify the numbers before using for decisions. Types of simulations available include: 1. Changed master production schedule: A. Material impact. B. Capacity impact. C. Financial impact. D. Marketing impact. 2. Make/Buy simulations. 3. Different forecast — same MPS. 4. Sales promotions — same or different MPS. 5. New product introductions.

Darryl Landvater
MANUFACTURING SOFTWARE SYSTEMS, INC.
P.O. Box 278
Williston, Vermont 05495
(802) 878-5254